SCOTLAND'S GARDENS SCHEME 1996

Contents

FRONT COVER PHOTOGRAPH

Camellia x williamsii "Donation", a hybrid between Camellia japonica and
C. saluensis, is perhaps the most beautiful Camellia bred this century.
It is probably the most reliable Camellia for the Scottish garden.
Photographed at Logan Botanic Garden, Wigtownshire, by Sidney J Clarke, ARPS,
Principal Photographer at the Royal Botanic Garden, Edinburgh.

Printed by Mackenzie & Storrie Ltd. , Edinburgh

CHAIRMAN'S MESSAGE

All over Scotland from early March to October each year, gardens of every size open for charity under the auspices of Scotland's Gardens Scheme. Last year we passed the £3,000,000 mark raised since the Scheme started in 1931 which is a fact to be very proud of and proof of its success.

To those of you reading this book for the first time, you will see how our beneficiaries use the money raised by all our generous owners and the many different charities which benefit from the 40% which owners may give to the charity of their choice. You will also see the names of the many voluntary organisers, area organisers and treasurers who so generously give their time to help organise the Scheme. In fact, SGS has only two paid members of staff, which I think is remarkable, considering how much work there is to do and how efficiently it is done.

This year I should like to thank the editors of daily newspapers, weekly local papers, and all varieties of magazines which carry details of our openings free of charge. There is little doubt that their help has greatly contributed to the sums raised.

Carry this booklet in your car, watch for the yellow Garden Open signs and you will add immeasurable pleasure to your travels and help many charities at the same time.

Barbara Findlay

❖ ❖

SCOTLAND'S GARDENS SCHEME HISTORY

Scotland's Gardens Scheme was founded on 23rd March 1931 at a garden owners' meeting called to help raise £2,000 which the Queen's Nursing Institute needed to fund the rapid expansion of district nursing. The Queen Mother, then the Duchess of York, lent her support, while King George V promised that the Balmoral gardens would open for the Scheme, with a generous annual contribution still being made today.

Under the inaugural chairmanship of the Countess of Minto, a central committee with a network of volunteer organisers throughout Scotland was formed, much the shape of the Scheme today. £1,000 was raised in the first year, double that in the next, and by 1939 over £22,000 was contributed in one shilling entrance fees. Even during the war years the proceeds increased, helped by flower and plant stalls, and through the provision of teas - without sugar.

Although the training duties of the Queen's Nursing Institute were taken over by the National Health Service, many elderly nurses then and now still receive our support. In 1952 the Gardens Fund of the National Trust for Scotland became our other main beneficiary, so that we could help to preserve the many gardens of historical importance in Scotland. Both our principal beneficiaries have contributed articles to this handbook, explaining in detail how important our contributions are and how they are used.

In 1961 it was agreed that all garden owners might select a registered charity to which up to 40% of the gross takings from their garden opening could be donated. This benefits over 140 different charities each year and is unique to Scotland's Gardens Scheme.

Over the years Scotland's Gardens Scheme has enabled millions of people to enjoy the beautiful and often 'never before seen' gardens of Scotland - with your help we hope that this will continue for many years to come.

A MESSAGE FROM
THE QUEEN'S NURSING INSTITUTE, SCOTLAND

Once again we are deeply indebted to all those involved with Scotland's Gardens Scheme for the donation of £45,344 made to the Institute in 1995 which has enabled us to fund new schemes bringing **Nursing Care into the Home.**

Our two year scheme with **Marie Curie Cancer Care Scotland and Scottish Motor Neurone Disease Association** has been successfully completed; the final report was most illuminating and has been widely circulated. After unavoidable delays, four major new schemes are underway, all involving nursing in the home. These are working in conjunction with **Children's Hospice Association Scotland** (Rachel House, Kinross, outreach facility), **Chest Heart & Stroke Scotland** (Stirling Stroke Rehabilitation), **Alzheimer Scotland** (North Grampian Dementia Care) and **Edinburgh Sick Children's Hospital** (Diabetic Nurse). Another five minor projects are being funded in Glasgow, Dumfries, Alloa and Lothian - all assisting community nurses to improve the quality of care.

A leaflet outlining the work of the Queen's Nursing Institute Scotland is available from the Institute. We are fully aware that our ability not only to assist hard-pressed nurses with these projects, but also to support retired Queen's Nurses and make a positive contribution to the education of community nurses, is dependent on the generosity of all those who assist Scotland's Gardens Scheme in so many different ways.

Last year I expressed the hope that the sun would shine on all your gardens. It did! I hope it will continue to do so but perhaps, this year, accompanied by modest rainfall overnight.

George Preston
Secretary & Treasurer

The Queen's Nursing Institute
31 Castle Terrace, Edinburgh EH1 2EL

A MESSAGE TO GARDEN OWNERS FROM

♛ The National Trust for Scotland

I am very grateful to Scotland's Gardens Scheme for giving me the opportunity in this most interesting and informative booklet to say a very sincere thank you, on behalf of The National Trust for Scotland, to garden owners who, through their love of gardening and their pleasure of sharing this with others, contribute so much to a wide range of charities including this Trust.

For most of us the summer of 1995 was long, hot and dry. These are not necessarily ideal gardening conditions, especially in this country! So I am full of admiration for all of those owners who toiled in the heat to maintain the extremely high standard we have come to expect - and enjoy - of gardens in Scotland's Gardens Scheme.

The Trust is extremely grateful to those garden owners who have contributed directly to the Trust's Gardens Fund. I cannot tell you how much this is appreciated. With so many gardens of our own open to the public - some all year round - these contributions will help us in a great many ways.

I hope that all those who read this book will be able to visit many of the private gardens and Trust gardens in 1996. The experience will, I am sure, enthral and delight and, I hope, perhaps encourage others to participate in opening their own gardens for Scotland's Gardens Scheme and/or to join The National Trust for Scotland.

Douglas Dow
Director

The Gardeners' Royal Benevolent Society in Scotland

An Exempt Charity Registered under the Industrial & Provident Societies Act 1974. Number 15408B.

The GRBS currently assists some 500 beneficiaries with regular quarterly payments and invites applications from other retired gardeners and their spouses interested in becoming a beneficiary of the Society. Help is also given from the Good Samaritan Fund for unexpected expenses and special needs. Sheltered housing is offered in three locations in England and Red Oaks, the Society's home at Henfield in Sussex, offers residential and nursing care. In Scotland, Netherbyres near Eyemouth, which opened its doors to retired gardeners in 1993 is now well established.

In 1995 the number of Regional Organisers in Scotland rose to five, thus bringing the Gardeners' Royal Benevolent Society to many more people throughout the country. Please look out for the Society's Regional Organisers at gardening events during the year, they would be very glad to meet you.

For further information please contact Miss May Wardlaw, GRBS Regional Organiser, c/o SGS, 31 Castle Terrace, Edinburgh EH1 2EL *or* Colin Bunce, Chief Executive, The Gardeners' Royal Benevolent Society, Bridge House, 139 Kingston Road, Leatherhead, Surrey KT22 7NT. Tel: 01372 373962 Fax: 01372 362575.

THE ROYAL GARDENERS' ORPHAN FUND

Registered Charity No. 248746

The assistance we are able to offer, not only to orphaned children, but also those in particular need, is greatly appreciated and needed by the families who qualify for our help. We are able to offer support to orphaned children by way of regular maintenance allowances and to help those in need with grants towards the purchase of such essential items as clothing, beds and bedding.

Over the past year we have been helping sixteen children in Scotland who vary in age from four to seventeen, and we are sincerely grateful for the donation we receive each year from Scotland's Gardens Scheme which helps to make this assistance possible.

Should you wish for any further details of our work, or perhaps know of a child who may qualify for our assistance, please contact our Secretary, Mrs Kate Wallis.

The Royal Gardeners' Orphan Fund
48 St Albans Road
Codicote, Hitchen
Herts SG4 8UT
Tel: 01438 820783

GENERAL INFORMATION

Houses are not open unless specifically stated; where the house or part of the house is shown, an additional charge is usually made.

Lavatories. Private gardens do not normally have outside lavatories. Regrettably, for security reasons, owners have been advised not to admit visitors into their houses.

Dogs. Unless otherwise stated, dogs are usually admitted, but only if kept on a lead. They are not admitted to houses.

Teas. When teas are available this is indicated in the text. An extra charge is usually made for refreshments.

Professional Photographers. No photographs taken in a garden may be used for sale or reproduction without the prior permission of the garden owner.

 ♿ Denotes gardens suitable for wheelchairs.

\#   Denotes gardens opening for the first time or re-opening after several years.

The National Trust for Scotland. Members are requested to note that where a National Trust property has allocated an opening day to Scotland's Gardens Scheme which is one of its own normal opening days, members can gain entry on production of their Trust membership card , although donations to Scotland's Gardens Scheme will be most welcome.

Children. All children must be accompanied by an adult.

SCOTLAND'S GARDENS SCHEME
Charity No. SC011337

We welcome gardens large and small and also groups of gardens.
If you would like information on how to open your garden for charity please contact us at the address below.

**SCOTLAND'S GARDENS SCHEME,
31 CASTLE TERRACE, EDINBURGH EH1 2EL**

Telephone: 0131 229 1870   Fax: 0131 229 0443

NAME & ADDRESS: (Block capitals please) ....

....

....

.... Post Code ....

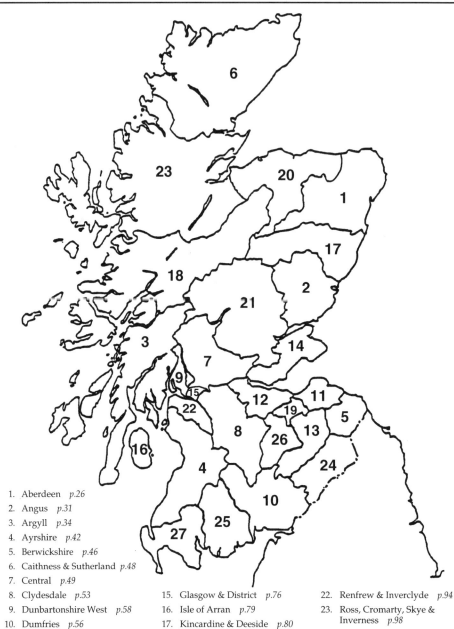

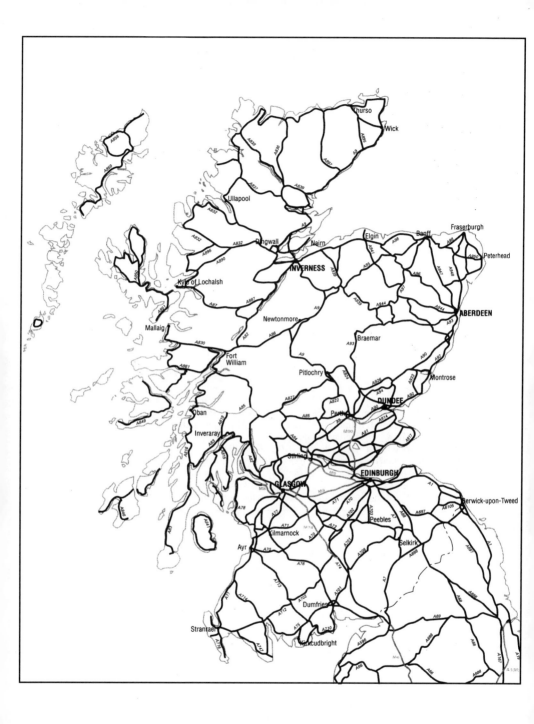

THE GARDENS LISTED BELOW OPEN FOR SCOTLAND'S GARDENS SCHEME ON A REGULAR BASIS, OR BY APPOINTMENT.

Full details are given in the District List of Gardens

ABERDEEN

23 Don Street, Old Aberdeen   *Daily April-Oct by appointment: 01224 487269*
Kildrummy Castle Gardens, Alford   *Daily April-October*
Nether Affloch Farmhouse, Dunecht   *June to September by appointment: 01330 860362*
Old Semeil Herb Garden, Strathdon   *May to August 10am - 5pm*
Pitmedden Garden, Pitmedden   *Daily May-September 10am - 5.30pm*

ANGUS

House of Pitmuies, Guthrie,   *Daily 1 April – 31 October 10am-5pm*

ARGYLL

Achnacloich, Connel   *Daily 1 April-31 October 10am - 6pm*
An Cala, Ellenabeich   *Daily 1 April-15 October 10am - 6pm*
Ardchattan Priory, North Connel   *Daily 1 April-30 October 9am - 9pm*
Ardkinglas Woodland Garden, Cairndow   *Daily all year*
Ardmaddy Castle, Balvicar   *Daily 1 April-31 October or by appt: 01852 300353*
Barguillean's 'Angus Garden', Taynuilt   *Daily all year*
#Cnoc-na-Garrie, by Lochgilphead   *By appointment: 01546 605327*
Coille Dharaich, Kilmelford   *By appointment: 01852 200285*
Crarae Glen Garden, Minard   *Daily April-October 9am - 6pm. Winter daylight hours*
Crinan Hotel Garden, Crinan   *Daily 30 April - 30 September*
Dalnaheish, Tayvallich   *April-September by appointment: 01546   870286*
Druimavuic House, Appin   *Daily 14 April-30 June 10am - 6 pm*
Druimneil House, Port Appin   *Daily 28 March-19 June 9am - 6pm*
#Eredine Woodland Garden, Lochaweside   *By appointment Spring - Autumn: 01866 844207*
Glenfeochan House Hotel, Kilmore   *Daily 15 March-31 October 10am - 6pm*
Jura House, Isle of Jura   *Open all year 9am - 5pm*
#Kildalloig, Campbeltown   *By appointment: 01586 553192*
Kinlochlaich House Gardens, Appin   *Open all year 9.30am-5.30pm or dusk (except Suns Oct-March)*
Mount Stuart, Isle of Bute   *1 May - 30 Sep.(not Tues & Thurs) 11am-5pm. Also Sat/Sun April & Oct.*
Tighnamara, Kilmelford   *By appointment spring - autumn: 01852 200224*
Torosay Castle & Gardens, Isle of Mull   *Open all year. Summer 9am - 7pm.Winter, sunrise - sunset*

AYRSHIRE

Blair, Dalry   *All year round*
Culzean Castle & Country Park   *Daily 1 April-31October 10.30am-5pm*

BERWICKSHIRE

Bughtrig, Leitholm   *June – September 11am-5pm or by appointment: 01890 840678*
The Hirsel, Coldstream   *Open daily all year reasonable daylight hours*
Manderston, Duns   *Sundays & Thursdays 9 May-29 September*

CENTRAL

Daldrishaig House, Aberfoyle   *May to September by appointment: 01877 382223*
Kilbryde Castle   *All year by appointment: 01786 823104*

DUMFRIES
Arbigland, Kirkbean   *Tuesdays-Sundays: May-September 2-6pm Also Bank Holiday Mondays*

DUNBARTONSHIRE WEST
Auchendarroch, Tarbet   *1 April – 30 June by appointment: 01301 702240*
Glenarn, Rhu   *Daily 21 March-21 June, Sunrise to Sunset*

EDINBURGH & WEST LOTHIAN
Newliston, Kirkliston   *Wednesdays-Sundays 1May- 2 June 2-6pm*

FIFE
Cambo House, Kingsbarns   *Daily all year 10am-5pm*
Mickelgarth, Aberdour   *20 May - 31 August by appointment: 01383 860796*

GLASGOW
Invermay, Cambuslang   *April – September by appointment: 0141 641 1632*

KINCARDINE & DEESIDE
Shooting Greens, Strachan   *28 April – 12 May by appointment: 01330 850221*

LOCHABER, BADENOCH & STRATHSPEY
Ardtornish, Lochaline   *Daily 1 April-31 October 10am-6pm*

MIDLOTHIAN
Arniston, Gorebridge   *Tuesdays, Thursdays & Sundays July-mid September*
Greenfield Lodge, Lasswade   *First Tuesdays of each month April-September incl. 2-5pm,*
                                 or by appointment: 0131 663 9338
#The Mill House, Temple   *Second Wednesday of each month April-September incl. 2-5pm*

PERTH AND KINROSS
Ardvorlich, Lochearnhead   *11 May - 9 June 2 - 6pm*
Bolfracks, Aberfeldy   *Daily 1 April-31 October 10am - 6pm*
Cluny House, Aberfeldy   *Daily 1 March-31 October 10am - 6pm*
Drummond Castle Gardens, Muthill   *Daily May-October 2 - 6pm,last entrance 5pm*
Scone Palace, Perth   *5 April-14 October 9.30am - 5pm*

RENFREW & INVERCLYDE
Mosswood, Kilmacolm   *May & June by appointment: 01505 872493*

ROSS, CROMARTY, SKYE & INVERNESS
Abriachan Garden Nursery, Loch Ness side   *February-November 9am - dusk*
Aigas House & Field Centre, by Beauly   *Daily mid June- September*
Attadale, Strathcarron   *1 April-1 Oct. 10am-1pm, not Sundays*
Brin School Fields, Flichity   *Daily June-Sept. 8.30am - 7pm, Sundays 2 - 5pm*
#Coiltie, Divach, Drumnadrochit   *Daily June-August 12-7pm*
Dunvegan Castle, Isle of Skye   *25 March-31 October 10am-5.30pm, last entry 5pm*
Glamaig, Isle of Skye   *Daily Easter to mid September*

Leckmelm Shrubbery & Arboretum by Ullapool   *Daily 1 April-30 September 10am - 6pm*
Sea View, Dundonnell   *Daily May - September*
Tournaig, Poolewe   *By appointment: 01445 781250 or 339*

ROXBURGH
Floors Castle, Kelso   *Daily Easter – end September 10.30am – 5.30pm,*
October: Sundays & Wednesdays 10.30am-4.30pm

STEWARTRY OF KIRKCUDBRIGHT
Corsock House, Castle Douglas   *Open by appointment: 01644 440250*

TWEEDDALE
Kailzie Gardens, Peebles   *Daily 23 March-19 October 11am-5.30pm*
Winter: Daylight hours, gardens only

WIGTOWN
Ardwell House Gardens, Ardwell   *Daily 1 April-30 September 10am-5pm*
Castle Kennedy & Lochinch Gardens   *Daily 1 April-30 September 10am-5pm*
Glenwhan, Dunragit   *Daily 1 April-30 September*
Whitehills, Newton Stewart   *Daily 1 April-31 October by appointment: 01671 102019*

PLANT SALES in 1996

If any garden has a plant sale on the opening day this is mentioned in the text. The following Plant Sales are held as 'special events' on their own and offer an opportunity to bring and buy. For further details see text.

Dunbartonshire West: THE HILL HOUSE, Helensburgh
Sunday 1st SEPTEMBER 11am - 5pm.

Edinburgh & West Lothian: KIRKNEWTON HOUSE, Kirknewton
Saturday 28th SEPTEMBER 11am - 4pm and
Sunday 29th SEPTEMBER 2 - 5pm.

Fife: HILL OF TARVIT, Cupar
Saturday 5th OCTOBER 10.30am - 4pm
Sunday 6th OCTOBER 2 - 5pm

Midlothian: OXENFOORD MAINS, Dalkeith
Sunday 13th OCTOBER 11am - 4pm

MONTHLY CALENDAR LIST

FEBRUARY

Dates to be announced
EDINBURGH & WEST LOTHIAN .... **DALMENY PARK,** South Queensferry
STEWARTY OF KIRKCUDBRIGHT .... **DANEVALE PARK,** Crossmichael

SUNDAY 11th FEBRUARY
RENFREW & INVERCLYDE .... **ARDGOWAN**, Inverkip   2 - 5pm

SUNDAY 25th FEBRUARY (provisionally)
FIFE .... **CAMBO HOUSE,** Kingsbarns   2 – 5pm

MARCH

SUNDAY 10th MARCH
MIDLOTHIAN .... **GREENFIELD LODGE,** Lasswade   2 – 5pm

SUNDAY 17th MARCH
CENTRAL .... **KILBRYDE CASTLE,** Dunblane   2 – 4pm
MIDLOTHIAN .... **PRESTONHALL,** Pathhead   2 - 5pm

SUNDAY 24th MARCH
MIDLOTHIAN .... **GREENFIELD LODGE,** Lasswade   2 – 5pm

SUNDAY 31st MARCH
GLASGOW & DISTRICT .... **#CALDERGLEN COUNTRY PARK** 5.30-8pm

APRIL

TUESDAY 2nd APRIL
MIDLOTHIAN .... **GREENFIELD LODGE,** Lasswade   2 – 5pm

WEDNESDAY 3rd APRIL
ARGYLL .... **#CNOC-NA-GARRIE,** by Lochgilphead   2 - 6pm

SUNDAY 7th APRIL
AYRSHIRE .... **CULZEAN CASTLE**
                                     & COUNTRY PARK   10.30am – 5pm

SATURDAY 13th APRIL

EDINBURGH & WEST LOTHIAN .... **THE TREFOIL CENTRE,** Gogarbank 2 - 5pm

SUNDAY 14th APRIL

CENTRAL	**KILBRYDE CASTLE,** Dunblane	2 - 5pm
EAST LOTHIAN	**WINTON HOUSE,** Pencaitland	2 - 6pm
EDINBURGH & WEST LOTHIAN	**DEAN GARDENS & ANN STREET,** Edinburgh	2 - 6pm
GLASGOW & DISTRICT	**GREENBANK GARDEN & HOUSE,** Clarkston	11am-5pm
MIDLOTHIAN	**ARNISTON,** Gorebridge	2-5.30pm
PERTH & KINROSS	**MEIKLEOUR HOUSE,** by Blairgowrie	2-5pm
RENFREW & INVERCLYDE	**FINLAYSTONE,** Langbank	2 - 5pm

SUNDAY 21st APRIL

ABERDEEN	**AUCHMACOY,** Ellon	1.30-4.30pm
BERWICKSHIRE	**NETHERBYRES,** Eyemouth	2 - 6pm
CENTRAL	**WEST PLEAN,** by Stirling	1.30-4.30pm
EDINBURGH & WEST LOTHIAN	**FOXHALL,** by Kirkliston	2-5.30pm
ETTRICK & LAUDERDALE	**BEMERSYDE,** Melrose	2 - 6pm
MIDLOTHIAN	**PRESTONHALL,** Pathhead	2 - 6pm

SATURDAY 27th APRIL

EDINBURGH & WEST LOTHIAN	**#REDHALL WALLED GARDEN,** Edinburgh	10am-3pm
ROSS, CROMARTY, SKYE & INVERNESS	**INVEREWE,** Poolewe	9.30am-sunset

SUNDAY 28th APRIL

ARGYLL	**YOUNGER BOTANIC GARDEN,** Benmore	10am-6pm
CENTRAL	**THE PASS HOUSE,** Kilmahog	2-5.30pm
DUNBARTONSHIRE WEST	**GLENARN,** Rhu	2-5.30pm
EDINBURGH & WEST LOTHIAN	**HETHERSETT,** Balerno	2-5.30pm
FIFE	**BARHAM,** Bow of Fife	12-4pm
KINCARDINE & DEESIDE	**SHOOTING GREENS,** Strachan	2 - 5pm
MIDLOTHIAN	**#NEWHALL,** Carlops	2 - 5pm
STEWARTRY OF KIRKCUDBRIGHT	**WALTON PARK,** Castle Douglas	2 - 5pm

---

MAY

WEDNESDAY 1st MAY

ARGYLL .... **#CNOC-NA-GARRIE,** by Lochgilphead   2 - 6pm

SUNDAY 5th MAY

AYRSHIRE	**CULZEAN CASTLE & COUNTRY PARK**	10.30am – 5pm
CENTRAL	**DUCHRAY CASTLE,** Aberfoyle	2 - 5pm
	KILBRYDE CASTLE, Dunblane	2 - 5pm
PERTH & KINROSS	**GLENDOICK,** Perth	2 - 5pm
TWEEDDALE	**DAWYCK BOTANIC GARDEN,** Stobo	10am-6pm

TUESDAY 7th MAY

MIDLOTHIAN	**GREENFIELD LODGE,** Lasswade	2 – 5pm

SATURDAY & SUNDAY 11th & 12th MAY

ARGYLL	**ARDUAINE,** Kilmelford	9.30-6pm
EDINBURGH & WEST LOTHIAN	**DR NEIL'S GARDEN,** Duddingston	2 - 5pm

SUNDAY 12th MAY

AYRSHIRE	**#PENKILL CASTLE,** near Girvan	2 - 5pm
DUNBARTONSHIRE WEST	**ASKIVAL,** Kilcreggan	2-5.30pm
EAST LOTHIAN	**TYNINGHAME,** Dunbar	2 - 6pm
FIFE	**CAMBO HOUSE,** Kingsbarns	2 - 5pm
	SALINE VILLAGE GARDENS	2 - 6pm
GLASGOW & DISTRICT	**60 CLEVEDEN DRIVE,** Kelvinside	2 - 5pm
PERTH & KINROSS	**BRANKLYN,** Perth	9.30am-sunset
	GLENDOICK, Perth	2 - 5pm
	MEIKLEOUR HOUSE, by Blairgowrie	2-5pm
ROSS, CROMARTY, SKYE & INVERNESS	**ALLANGRANGE,** Munlochy	2-5.30pm

SATURDAY & SUNDAY 18th & 19th MAY

ARGYLL	**KYLES of BUTE SMALL GARDENS**	2 - 6pm

SUNDAY 19th MAY

ANGUS	**KINNAIRD CASTLE,** Brechin	2 - 5pm
ARGYLL	**ARDKINGLAS HOUSE,** Cairndow	11am-6pm
AYRSHIRE	**AUCHINCRUIVE,** Ayr	1-5.30pm
DUMFRIES	**THE CRICHTON ,** Dumfries	2 - 5pm
DUNBARTONSHIRE WEST	**AUCHENDARROCH,** Tarbet	2-5.30pm
EAST LOTHIAN	**LENNOXLOVE,** Haddington	12-5pm
EDINBURGH & WEST LOTHIAN	**COLINTON GARDENS,** Edinburgh	2 - 5pm
FIFE	**MICKLEGARTH,** Aberdour	2 - 5pm
PERTH & KINROSS	**GLENDOICK,** Perth	2 - 5pm
	ROSSIE, by Bridge of Earn	2 - 6pm
	STOBHALL, by Perth	2 - 6pm

WEDNESDAY 22nd MAY

AYRSHIRE	#KELBURN CASTLE	
	& COUNTRY PARK, Fairlie	6 - 8pm

SATURDAY 25th MAY

ARGYLL	#EREDINE WOODLAND GARDEN,	
	Lochaweside	11am-6pm
DUNBARTONSHIRE WEST	GEILSTON HOUSE, Cardross	2-5.30pm
ROSS, CROMARTY,		
SKYE & INVERNESS	HOUSE OF GRUINARD, by Laide	2 - 6pm

SATURDAY & SUNDAY 25th & 26th MAY

ARGYLL	COLINTRAIVE GARDENS	2 - 6pm
RENFREW & INVERCLYDE	RENFREW CENTRAL NURSERY,	
	Paisley	1 - 5pm

SUNDAY 26th MAY

ABERDEEN	CULQUOICH, Alford	1.30-5pm
ANGUS	BRECHIN CASTLE	2-5.30pm
	KINNETTLES HOUSE, byForfar	2 - 6pm
AYRSHIRE	ASHCRAIG, Skelmorlie	2-5.30pm
CENTRAL	#AIRTHREY Estate, Bridge of Allan	2-5.30pm
	KILBRYDE CASTLE, Dunblane	2 - 5pm
	THE PASS HOUSE, Kilmahog	2-5.30pm
DUMFRIES	#DRUMCLYER, Irongray	2 - 5pm
DUNBARTONSHIRE WEST	ROSS PRIORY, Gartocharn	2 - 6pm
EAST LOTHIAN	STENTON VILLAGE	2 - 6pm
FIFE	WHITEHILL, Aberdour	2-5.30pm
KINCARDINE & DEESIDE	#INCHMARLO HOUSE., Banchory	1.30-5pm
LOCHABER, BADENOCH		
& STRATHSPEY	ACHNACARRY, Spean Bridge	2-5.30pm
	ARDTORNISH, Lochaline	2 - 6pm
PERTH & KINROSS	GLENDOICK, Perth	2 - 5pm
RENFREW & INVERCLYDE	#CROSSWAYS, Bishopton	1 - 5pm
ROSS, CROMARTY,		
SKYE & INVERNESS	LAGGAN HOUSE, Scaniport	2 - 5pm
STEWARTRY OF KIRKCUDBRIGHT	BARNHOURIE MILL, Colvend	2 - 5pm
TWEEDDALE	HAYSTOUN, Peebles	2-5.30pm
WIGTOWN	LOGAN BOTANIC GARDEN	10am-6pm
	#MONREITH HOUSE GARDEN,	
	Port William	10am-5pm

MONDAY 27th MAY

BERWICKSHIRE	MANDERSTON, Duns	2-5.30pm

WEDNESDAY 29th MAY

ROSS, CROMARTY,		
SKYE & INVERNESS	TOURNAIG, Poolewe	2 - 6pm

JUNE

SATURDAY 1st JUNE

ARGYLL...**#EREDINE WOODLAND GARDEN,**
                                        Lochaweside   11am-6pm
ROSS, CROMARTY,
SKYE & INVERNESS...................................**ATTADALE**, Strathcarron   2 - 6pm

SATURDAY & SUNDAY 1st & 2nd JUNE

EAST LOTHIAN ....**DIRLETON VILLAGE**   2 - 6pm
PERTH & KINROSS ....**#KINROSS PRIVATE**
                                        SPRING GARDENS   2-5.30pm

SUNDAY 2nd JUNE

ABERDEEN ....**DUNECHT HOUSE GARDENS**   1 - 5pm
                                        KILDRUMMY CASTLE
                                        GARDENS, Alford   10am-5pm
ANGUS ....**CORTACHY CASTLE**, Kirriemuir   2 - 6pm
AYRSHIRE ....**DOONHOLM,** Ayr   2-5.30pm
CENTRAL...**#CALLANDER LODGE,** Callander   2-5pm
                                        OLD BALLIKINRAIN, Balfron   11am-5pm
DUMFRIES ....**DALSWINTON HOUSE,** Auldgirth   2 - 5pm
DUNBARTONSHIRE WEST ....**THE LINN GARDEN,** Cove   2 - 6pm
FIFE ....**FALKLAND PALACE GARDEN**   2 - 5pm
GLASGOW & DISTRICT ....**#ACRE VALLEY HOUSE,** Torrance   2 - 5pm
LOCHABER, BADENOCH
    & STRATHSPEY ....**ARD-DARAICH,** Ardgour   2 - 5pm
MIDLOTHIAN ....**PENICUIK HOUSE,** Penicuik   2-5.30pm
MORAY & NAIRN ....**#CARESTOWN STEADING,**Deskford 2-5pm
PERTH & KINROSS ....**GREENACRES,** Logiealmond   2 - 5pm
                                        KENNACOIL HOUSE, Dunkeld   2 - 6pm
RENFREW & INVERCLYDE ....**CARRUTH PLANT SALE,**
                                        Bridge of Weir   2 - 5pm
ROXBURGH..**MERTOUN**, St Boswells   2 - 6pm
STEWARTRY OF KIRKCUDBRIGHT ....**CORSOCK HOUSE,** Castle Douglas   2 - 5pm
TWEEDDALE ....**HALLMANOR,** Kirkton Manor   2 - 6pm
WIGTOWN ....**WHITEHILLS,** Newton Stewart   2 - 5pm

TUESDAY 4th JUNE

MIDLOTHIAN ....**GREENFIELD LODGE**, Lasswade   2 -5 pm

WEDNESDAY 5th JUNE

ARGYLL...**#CNOC-NA-GARRIE,** by Lochgilphead   2 - 6pm
MORAY & WEST BANFF ....**REVACK,** Grantown-on-Spey   10am-6pm

THURSDAY 6th JUNE

ROSS, CROMARTY, ... **DUNDONNELL,**
SKYE & INVERNESS   by Little Loch Broom   2-5.30pm

SATURDAY 8th JUNE

ROSS, CROMARTY, ... **LOCHALSH WOODLAND GARDEN,**
SKYE & INVERNESS   Balmacara   1-5.30pm

SATURDAY & SUNDAY 8th & 9th JUNE

ARGYLL... **ARDENTALLEN GARDENS,**
                                          Lerags   2 - 6pm

SUNDAY 9th JUNE

ABERDEEN .... **DUNECHT HOUSE GARDENS**   1 - 5pm
AYRSHIRE .... **BARNWEIL**, Craigie   2-5.30pm
CENTRAL.. **DUNTREATH CASTLE,** Blanefield   2 - 5pm
                                          KILBRYDE CASTLE, Dunblane   2 - 5pm
DUMFRIES .... **CRAIGIEBURN**, Moffat   12.30-8pm
                                          #CRAIGIELANDS MILL, Beattock   2 - 5pm
EAST LOTHIAN .... **HUMBIE HOUSE,** Humbie   2 - 5pm
FIFE... **GILSTON**, Largoward   1.30-6pm
MIDLOTHIAN .... **#NEWHALL,** Carlops   2 - 6pm
MORAY & NAIRN .... **DALLAS LODGE**, by Forres   2 - 6pm
                                          DELNESMUIR, Nairn   2 - 5pm
PERTH & KINROSS .... **CLOQUHAT GARDENS,**
                                          Bridge of Cally   2 - 6pm
                                          MEIKLEOUR HOUSE, by Blairgowrie 2-5pm
RENFREW & INVERCLYDE .... **PARKLEA NURSERY,**
                                          Port Glasgow   11am-4pm
ROSS, CROMARTY,
SKYE & INVERNESS.................................... **BRAHAN**, Dingwall   2-5.30pm
TWEEDDALE .... **STOBO WATER GARDEN,** Peebles   2 - 5pm

WEDNESDAY 12th JUNE

CENTRAL.. **DALDRISHAIG HOUSE,**
                                          Aberfoyle   2 - 5pm
ROSS, CROMARTY, ... **DUNDONNELL,**
SKYE & INVERNESS   by Little Loch Broom   2-5.30pm

SATURDAY & SUNDAY 15th & 16th JUNE

ARGYLL... **COILLE DHARAICH**, Kilmelford   2 - 6pm
                                          TIGHNAMARA, Kilmelford   2 - 6pm
EDINBURGH & WEST LOTHIAN .... **ARTHUR LODGE**, Edinburgh   2 - 5pm

SUNDAY 16th JUNE

ABERDEEN .... **TERTOWIE**, Clinterty   1 - 4pm
ANGUS .... **EDZELL VILLAGE &**
                                          EDZELL CASTLE   1.30-5.30pm
CENTRAL.. **THE BLAIR & GARDENS**
                                          IN BLAIRLOGIE   2 - 5pm

18

CLYDESDALE	**#DIPPOOLBANK COTTAGE,**	
	Carnwath	2 - 6pm
	LAWHEAD CROFT, Tarbrax	2 - 6pm
DUMFRIES	**DALGONAR,** Dunscore	2 - 5pm
EAST LOTHIAN	**STEVENSON HOUSE,** Haddington	2 - 6pm
EDINBURGH & WEST LOTHIAN	**KIRKNEWTON HOUSE,**	
	Kirknewton (to 21st June)	2 - 6pm
	#MILL LADE HOUSE, Edinburgh	2-5.30pm
FIFE	**CULROSS PALACE GARDEN**	11am-5pm
	MYRES CASTLE, Auchtermuchty	2 - 5pm
PERTH & KINROSS	**BRANKLYN,** Perth	9.30am-sunset
ROSS, CROMARTY,	**ALLANGRANGE,** Munlochy	2-5.30pm
SKYE & INVERNESS	**KYLLACHY,** Tomatin	2-5.30pm
STEWARTRY OF KIRKCUDBRIGHT	**CALLY GARDENS,** Gatehouse	10am-5.30pm
WIGTOWN	**BARGALY HOUSE,** Palnure	2 - 5pm

MONDAY 17th JUNE
EAST LOTHIAN	**GREYWALLS HOTEL,** Gullane	2 - 5pm

SATURDAY 22nd JUNE
CAITHNESS & SUTHERLAND	**DUNROBIN CASTLE &**	
	GARDENS	10.30am-5.30pm

SUNDAY 23rd JUNE
ABERDEEN	**HOWEMILL,** Craigievar	1.30 - 5pm
ANGUS	**RESWALLIE,** by Forfar	2 - 5.30pm
AYRSHIRE	**SWALLOW HA',** Symington	2 - 6pm
CENTRAL	**#THE WALLED GARDEN,**	
	GEAN HOUSE, Alloa	2 - 5pm
CLYDESDALE	**NEMPHLAR GARDEN TRAIL,**	
	Lanark	2-5.30pm
EAST LOTHIAN	**BOWERHOUSE,** Dunbar	2 - 6pm
FIFE	**BALCASKIE,** Pittenweem	2 - 6pm
	HILL OF TARVIT, Cupar	12.30 - 5pm
GLASGOW & DISTRICT	**KITTOCH MILL,** Carmunnock	2 - 5pm
	WHITEMOSS HOUSE,	
	East Kilbride	2 - 5pm
KINCARDINE & DEESIDE	**CRATHES CASTLE,** Banchory	2 - 5pm
MORAY & NAIRN	**GORDONSTOUN,** Duffus	2 - 5.30pm
PERTH & KINROSS	**#KIRKTON CRAIG,** Abernyte	2 - 5pm
RENFREW, INVERCLYDE	**LUNDERSTON,** Ardgowan	2 - 5pm
STEWARTRY OF KIRKCUDBRIGHT	**SOUTHWICK HOUSE,** Dalbeattie	2 - 5pm

MONDAY 24th JUNE
EAST LOTHIAN	**GREYWALLS HOTEL,** Gullane	2 - 5pm

WEDNESDAY 26th JUNE

EDINBURGH & WEST LOTHIAN	**MALLENY HOUSE GARDEN,**	
	Balerno	2 - 5pm
	#REDHALL WALLED GARDEN,	
	Edinburgh	10am-3pm
PERTH & KINROSS	**LUDE**, Blair Atholl	11am-5pm

SATURDAY 29th JUNE

ANGUS	**HOUSE OF DUN,** Montrose	12.30-5pm

SATURDAY & SUNDAY 29th & 30th JUNE

EAST LOTHIAN	**INVERESK,** near Musselburgh	2-5.30pm
EDINBURGH	**#SWANSTON GARDENS**	2 - 5pm
FIFE..	**BARHAM,** Bow of Fife	2 -5.30pm
TWEEDDALE	**CRINGLETIE HOUSE HOTEL**,	
	Eddleston	2 - 5pm

SUNDAY 30th JUNE

ABERDEEN	**STATION COTTAGE,** Gartly	2 - 5pm
ANGUS ....,,,,,,,,,,	**NEWTONMILL HOUSE,** Edzell	2-5.30pm
CENTRAL..	**COLZIUM WALLED GARDEN,**	
	Kilsyth	2 - 5pm
	KILBRYDE CASTLE, Dunblane	2 - 5pm
CLYDESDALE	**STONYPATH,** Dunsyre	2 - 6pm
DUMFRIES	**#SKAIRFIELD,** Hightae, Lockerbie	2 - 5pm
FIFE..	**#46 SOUTH STREET,**	
	St Andrews	11.30am-5.30pm
	ST ANDREWS BOTANIC	
	GARDEN	10am-6pm
ISLE OF ARRAN	**DOUGARIE**	2 - 5pm
LOCHABER, BADENOCH	**RALIA LODGE & SMALL GARDENS**	
& STRATHSPEY	**in NEWTONMORE**	2 - 5pm
ROXBURGH...	**BENRIG, BENRIG COTTAGE,**	
	MANSFIELD HOUSE	
	& STABLE HOUSE, St Boswells	2 - 6pm

JULY

TUESDAY 2nd JULY

MIDLOTHIAN	**GREENFIELD LODGE,** Lasswade	2 - 5pm

WEDNESDAY 3rd JULY

ARGYLL..	**#CNOC-NA-GARRIE,** by Lochgilphead	2 - 6pm
PERTH & KINROSS	**LUDE**, Blair Atholl	11am-5pm

THURSDAY 4th JULY

ROSS, CROMARTY,
SKYE & INVERNESS .... DUNDONNELL, Little Loch Broom 2-5.30pm

FRIDAY 5th JULY

ETTRICK & LAUDERDALE .... #THE OLD MANSE,
Legerwood   6-8.30pm

SATURDAY 6th JULY

ANGUS .... BARNHILL ROCK GARDEN,
Broughty Ferry   1 - 4pm

SUNDAY 7th JULY

ABERDEEN .... OLD MAYEN, Rothiemay   2 - 6pm
ANGUS .... BRECHIN CASTLE, Brechin   2-5.30pm
                                                         GLAMIS CASTLE   10.30am-5.30pm
BERWICKSHIRE .... BUGHTRIG, near Leitholm   2.30-5pm
                                                         CHARTERHALL, Duns   2 - 5pm
CENTRAL.. BANKHEAD & PARK HOUSE,
Blair Drummond   2 - 5pm
CLYDESDALE .... CARMICHAEL MILL,
Hyndford Bridge   2 - 5pm
EAST LOTHIAN .... FORBES LODGE, Gifford   2 - 6pm
ETTRICK & LAUDERDALE .... CHAPEL-on-LEADER, Earlston   2 - 6pm
FIFE .... HILTON HOUSE, Cupar   2.30 - 5pm
                                                         KELLIE CASTLE, Pittenweem   1.30 - 5pm
GLASGOW & DISTRICT .... BYSTONE MEWS, Busby   2 - 5pm
KINCARDINE & DEESIDE .... DRUM CASTLE, Drumoak   1.30 - 5pm
RENFREW & INVERCLYDE .... #UPLAWMOOR GARDENS   2 - 6pm
STEWARTRY OF KIRKCUDBRIGHT .... #KIRKCUDBRIGHT GARDENS   2 - 5pm

MONDAY 8th JULY

EAST LOTHIAN .... GREYWALLS HOTEL, Gullane   2 - 5pm

WEDNESDAY 10th JULY

ISLE OF ARRAN .... BRODICK CASTLE &
                                                         COUNTRY PARK   10am-5pm
PERTH & KINROSS .... LUDE, Blair Atholl   11am-5pm
ROSS, CROMARTY,
SKYE & INVERNESS.................................... DUNDONNELL, Little Loch Broom 2-5.30pm

SUNDAY 14th JULY

ABERDEEN .... 23 DON STREET, Old Aberdeen   1.30-6pm
                                                         #KIRKSTILE HOUSE, Gartly   2 - 5pm
                                                         PITMEDDEN GARDENS,
Pitmedden   1.30 - 5pm
CENTRAL.. KILBRYDE CASTLE, Dunblane   2 - 5pm
CLYDESDALE .... BIGGAR PARK, Biggar   2 - 6pm
DUNBARTONSHIRE WEST .... GEILSTON HOUSE, Cardross   2-5.30pm

EAST LOTHIAN	**LUFFNESS**, Aberlady	2 - 6pm
ETTRICK & LAUDERDALE	**MELLERSTAIN**, Gordon	12.30-6.30pm
FIFE	**BALCARRES**, Colinsburgh	2 - 5pm
KINCARDINE & DEESIDE	**#GLASSEL LODGE,** Banchory	2 - 5pm
RENFREW & INVERCLYDE	**#BRIDGE OF WEIR GARDENS**	2 - 5pm
ROSS, CROMARTY,	**ABERCHALDER LODGE,** Invergarry	2 - 6pm
	ALLANGRANGE, Munlochy	2-5.30pm
ROXBURGH	**CORBET TOWER,** Morebattle	2 - 6pm
STEWARTRY OF KIRKCUDBRIGHT	**ARGRENNAN HOUSE,**	
	Castle Douglas	2 - 5pm
WIGTOWN	**#NEW LUCE VILLAGE GARDENS**	2 - 5pm

WEDNESDAY 17th JULY

CAITHNESS & SUTHERLAND	**CASTLE OF MEY**	2 - 6pm
PERTH & KINROSS	**LUDE**, Blair Atholl	11am-5pm
ROSS, CROMARTY, SKYE		
& INVERNESS	**HOUSE OF GRUINARD,** by Laide	2 - 6pm

THURSDAY 18th JULY

AYRSHIRE	**CULZEAN CASTLE**	
	& COUNTRY PARK	10.30am-5pm

SATURDAY & SUNDAY 20th & 21st JULY

FIFE	**CRAIL GARDENS**	2 - 6pm

SUNDAY 21st JULY

ABERDEEN	**CANDACRAIG NURSERY GARDEN,**	
	Strathdon	2 - 6pm
	LEITH HALL, Kennethmont	1.30-5pm
ARGYLL	**ARDCHATTAN PRIORY FETE**, N.Connel	
BERWICKSHIRE	**NETHERBYRES,** Eyemouth	2 – 6pm
CLYDESDALE	**#DIPPOOLBANK COTTAGE**,	
	Carnwath	2 - 6pm
	LAWHEAD CROFT, Tarbrax	2 - 6pm
EDINBURGH & WEST LOTHIAN	**BELGRAVE CRESCENT**, Edinburgh	2 - 5pm
FIFE	**LATHRISK & OLD LATHRISK,**	
	Freuchie	2-5.30pm
KINCARDINE & DEESIDE	**HOUSE OF STRACHAN,** Banchory	2 - 5pm
MORAY & NAIRN	**DRUMMUIR CASTLE GARDEN**,	
	by Keith	2 - 5pm
PERTH & KINROSS	**BORELAND,** Killin	2-5.30pm
RENFREW & INVERCLYDE	**ELDERSLIE GARDENS**	2 - 5pm
ROXBURGH	**MONTEVIOT**, Jedburgh	2 - 5pm
STEWARTRY OF KIRKCUDBRIGHT	**HENSOL**, Mossdale	2 - 5pm

WEDNESDAY 24th JULY

PERTH & KINROSS	**LUDE**, Blair Atholl	11am-5pm

THURSDAY 25th JULY

CAITHNESS & SUTHERLAND .... **CASTLE OF MEY**   2 - 6pm

SATURDAY 27th JULY

CAITHNESS & SUTHERLAND .... **HOUSE OF TONGUE,** Tongue   2 - 6pm

SUNDAY 28th JULY

ABERDEEN .... **CASTLE FRASER,** Kemnay   2 - 5pm
ANGUS .... **NEWTYLE VILLAGE**   1.30-5.30pm
ARGYLL.. **#KILDALLOIG,** Campbeltown   2 - 6pm
AYRSHIRE .... **CARNELL,** Hurlford   2-5.30pm
CENTRAL....................................... **ORCHARDLEA HOUSE,** Callander 2 - 5pm
CLYDESDALE .... **BAITLAWS,** Lamington   2 - 6pm
                                         GLENBRECK, Coulter   2 - 6pm
KINCARDINE & DEESIDE .... **BALMANNO,** Marykirk   2-5.30pm
                                         DOUNESIDE HOUSE, Tarland   2 - 5pm
                                         GLENBERVIE HOUSE, Drumlithie 2 - 5pm
MIDLOTHIAN .... **#BORTHWICK CASTLE HOTEL,**
                                         Borthwick   2 - 6pm
ROSS, CROMARTY, SKYE
  & INVERNESS .... **INVEREWE,** Poolewe   9.30am-sunset
TWEEDDALE .... **PORTMORE,** Eddleston   2 - 5pm

WEDNESDAY 31st JULY

PERTH & KINROSS .... **LUDE,** Blair Atholl   11am-5pm

---

AUGUST

SATURDAY & SUNDAY 3rd & 4th AUGUST

AYRSHIRE .... **BARR VILLAGE GARDENS**   1 - 5pm

SUNDAY 4th AUGUST

ABERDEEN .... **ESSLEMONT,** Ellon   1.30-5pm
                                                      GLENKINDIE HOUSE, Alford   1 - 5pm
AYRSHIRE .... **SKELDON,** Dalrymple   2 - 6pm
CENTRAL... **OLD BALLIKINRAIN,** Balfron 2 - 5pm
CLYDESDALE .... **CULTER ALLERS,** Coulter   2 - 6pm
EDINBURGH & WEST LOTHIAN .... **SUNTRAP,** Gogarbank   2 - 5pm
ETTRICK & LAUDERDALE .... **ABBOTSFORD,** Melrose   2-5.30pm
FIFE .... **FALKLAND PALACE GARDEN**   1.30 - 5pm
GLASGOW & DISTRICT .... **SIX FATHOMS,** Eaglesham   2 - 5pm
PERTH & KINROSS .... **BLAIRGOWRIE & RATTRAY**   1 - 6pm
                                                      DRUMMOND CASTLE
                                                      GARDENS, Muthill   2 - 6pm

ROXBURGH .... **YETHOLM VILLAGE GARDENS**   2 - 6pm
STEWARTRY OF KIRKCUDBRIGHT .... **THREAVE SCHOOL OF**
GARDENING, Castle Douglas   9am-5.30pm

TUESDAY 6th AUGUST
MIDLOTHIAN .... **GREENFIELD LODGE**, Lasswade   2 - 5pm

WEDNESDAY 7th AUGUST
ARGYLL...#**CNOC-NA-GARRIE,** by Lochgilphead   2 - 6pm
ISLE OF ARRAN .... **BRODICK CASTLE &**
COUNTRY PARK   10am-5pm
PERTH & KINROSS .... **LUDE**, Blair Atholl   11am-5pm
ROSS, CROMARTY, SKYE
& INVERNESS .... **TOURNAIG**, Poolewe   2 - 6pm

SATURDAY & SUNDAY 10th & 11th AUGUST
EDINBURGH & WEST LOTHIAN .... **DR NEIL'S GARDEN**, Duddingston 2 - 5pm
FIFE .... **PITTENWEEM GARDENS**   2-5.30pm

SUNDAY 11th AUGUST
ANGUS .... **KINPURNIE CASTLE,** Newtyle   2 - 6pm
AYRSHIRE ....'............ **BLAIRQUHAN**, Straiton   1.30-4.30pm
CAITHNESS & SUTHERLAND .... **LANGWELL**, Berriedale   2 - 6pm
CENTRAL... **KILBRYDE CASTLE**, Dunblane   2 - 5pm
EDINBURGH & WEST LOTHIAN .... **SOUTH QUEENSFERRY &**
DALMENY   1 - 6pm
GLASGOW & DISTRICT .... #**GLASGOW BOTANIC GARDEN**   12-4.45pm
PERTH & KINROSS .... **CLUNIEMORE**, Pitlochry   2 - 5pm
MEGGINCH CASTLE, Errol   2 - 5pm
STEWARTRY OF KIRKCUDBRIGHT .... **CALLY GARDENS**, Gatehouse 10am-5.30pm

SUNDAY 18th AUGUST
AYRSHIRE .... **LAGG HOUSE**, Dunure   2 - 5pm
CAITHNESS & SUTHERLAND .... **LANGWELL**, Berriedale   2 - 6pm
MIDLOTHIAN .... #**NEWHALL,** Carlops   2 - 6pm

SUNDAY 25th AUGUST
ABERDEEN .... **DUNECHT HOUSE GARDENS**   1 - 5pm
TILLYPRONIE, Tarland   2 - 5pm
ROSS, CROMARTY,
SKYE & INVERNESS.................................. #**GLENCALVIE,** by Ardgay   2 - 6p

MONDAY 26th AUGUST
BERWICKSHIRE .... **MANDERSTON**, Duns   2-5.30pm

SEPTEMBER

SUNDAY 1st SEPTEMBER

DUMFRIES .... **CRAIGIEBURN**, Moffat   12.30-8pm

DUNBARTONSHIRE WEST .... **THE HILL HOUSE**, Helensburgh

                                                           PLANT SALE   11am-5pm

TUESDAY 3rd SEPTEMBER

MIDLOTHIAN .... **GREENFIELD LODGE**, Lasswade   2 -5pm

WEDNESDAY 4th SEPTEMBER

ARGYLL .... **#CNOC-NA-GARRIE**, by Lochgilphead   2 - 6pm

SATURDAY 7th SEPTEMBER

CAITHNESS & SUTHERLAND .... **CASTLE OF MEY**   2 - 6pm

SUNDAY 8th SEPTEMBER

CENTRAL .... **KILBRYDE CASTLE**, Dunblane   2 - 5pm

SATURDAY & SUNDAY 21st & 22nd SEPTEMBER

PERTH & KINROSS .... **#BONSKEID HOUSE**,

                                                near Pitlochry   10.30-5pm

SUNDAY 22nd SEPTEMBER

LOCHABER, BADENOCH .... **ABERARDER**, Kinlochlaggan   2-5.30pm

& STRATHSPEY   **ARDVERIKIE**, Kinlochlaggan   2-5.30pm

SATURDAY & SUNDAY 28th & 29th SEPTEMBER

EDINBURGH & WEST LOTHIAN .... **SGS PLANT SALE,**

                                                KIRKNEWTON HOUSE, Kirknewton

                                                Saturday: 11am-4pm   Sunday: 2 - 5pm

---

OCTOBER

SATURDAY & SUNDAY 5th & 6th OCTOBER

FIFE .... **HILL OF TARVIT PLANT SALE**

                                                Saturday: 10.30am-4pm   Sunday: 2 - 5pm

SUNDAY 13th OCTOBER

CENTRAL .... **KILBRYDE CASTLE**, Dunblane   2 - 5pm

MIDLOTHIAN .... **SGS PLANT SALE,**

                                                OXENFOORD MAINS, Dalkeith 11am-4pm

SUNDAY 20th OCTOBER

PERTH & KINROSS .... **MEIKLEOUR HOUSE,** by Blairgowrie 2-5pm

ABERDEEN

Joint District Organisers:	**Mrs Robert Wolrige Gordon of Esslemont,** Esslemont House, Ellon AB41 8PA
	Mrs David James Duff, Hatton Castle, Turriff AB53 8ED
Area Organisers:	**Mrs D H W Brown,** Glenbogie, Rhynie, Huntly AB54 4JA
	Mrs W Bruce, Logie House, Ellon AB41 8LH
	Mrs G F Collie, Morkeu, Cults AB1 9PT
	Mrs F G Lawson, Asloun, Alford AB33 8NR
	Mrs A Robertson, Drumblade House, Huntly AB54 6ER
Hon. Treasurer:	**Mrs M Stewart-Richardson,** Manse of Glenbuchat, Strathdon AB36 8TN

DATES OF OPENING

23 Don Street, Old Aberdeen .... Daily April – October by appt.
Kildrummy Castle Gardens, Alford. .... Daily April – October
Nether Affloch Farmhouse, Dunecht .... June to September by appt.
Old Semeil Herb Garden, Strathdon .... May to August 10am - 5pm
Pitmedden Garden, Pitmedden .... Daily May – September 10am – 5.30pm

Auchmacoy, Ellon	Sunday 21 April	1.30 – 4.30pm
Culquoich, Alford	Sunday 26 May	1.30 – 5pm
Dunecht House Garden, Dunecht	Sunday 2 June	1 – 5pm
Kildrummy Castle Gardens, Alford	Sunday 2 June	10am – 5pm
Dunecht House Garden, Dunecht	Sunday 9 June	1 – 5pm
Tertowie Garden, Clinterty	Sunday 16 June	1 – 4pm
Howemill, Craigievar, Alford	Sunday 23 June	1.30-5pm
Station Cottage, Gartly	Sunday 30 June	2 - 5pm
Old Mayen, Rothiemay	Sunday 7 July	2 - 6pm
23 Don Street, Old Aberdeen	Sunday 14 July	1.30 – 6pm
Kirkstile House, Gartly	Sunday 14 July	2 – 5pm
Pitmedden Gardens, Pitmedden	Sunday 14 July	1.30 – 5pm
Candacraig Nursery Garden, Strathdon	Sunday 21 July	2 - 6pm
Leith Hall, Kennethmont, by Huntly	Sunday 21 July	1.30 – 5pm
Castle Fraser, Kemnay	Sunday 28 July	2 – 5pm
Esslemont, Ellon	Sunday 4 August	1.30 – 5pm
Glenkindie House, Alford	Sunday 4 August	1 – 5pm
Dunecht House Garden, Dunecht	Sunday 25 August	1 - 5pm
Tillypronie, Tarland	Sunday 25 August	2 - 5pm

26

23 DON STREET, Old Aberdeen ♿
(Miss M Mackechnie)
A secret small walled garden in historic Old Aberdeen. Recently developed using existing features giving a long established atmosphere. Wide range of unusual plants and old-fashioned roses. Small pool with aquatic plants. Teas with home baking. Park at St Machar Cathedral, short walk down Chanonry to Don Street, turn right. City plan ref: P7.
Admission £1.20 Children & OAPs 70p
OPEN APRIL TO OCTOBER BY APPOINTMENT Tel: 01224 487269.
SUNDAY 14th JULY 1.30 – 6pm
40% to Cat Protection League

AUCHMACOY, Ellon ♿
(Captain D W S Buchan)
Auchmacoy House policies feature an attractive display of tens of thousands of daffodils. Teas.
Admission £1.00 Children & OAPs 50p
SUNDAY 21st APRIL 1.30 – 4.30 pm
40% to Gordon Highlanders Museum Appeal

CANDACRAIG NURSERY GARDEN, Strathdon ♿ (limited)
The 3 acres within the walled garden contain a wild flower meadow and natural pond, formal herbaceous borders, terrace walk and cottage garden with a wide diversity of plants on view and for sale. The Victorian Gothic summerhouse, a great feature of the garden, is to be re-roofed and refurbished for completion by Spring 1996. Exhibitions staged throughout the summer. Display of patchwork on SGS open day when grounds of Candacraig House with fine specimen trees and interesting sculptures will also be open. Marquee teas. Free parking. Located ¼ m west of Rough Park garage on A944.
Admission to gardens £1.50 Concessions £1.00 Children free
SUNDAY 21st JULY 2 - 6pm
40% to Concern World Wide

CASTLE FRASER, Kemnay ♿
(The National Trust for Scotland)
Castle Fraser, one of the most spectacular of the Castles of Mar, belongs to the same period of native architectural achievements as Crathes Castle and Craigievar Castle. The walled garden has been fully restored by the Trust and forms a delightful adjunct to the Castle. Plant sales. Tea room. Trails, pipe band, stalls, competitions, horse and carriage rides. Near Kemnay, off B993.
Admission £1.60 Children £1.00
SUNDAY 28th JULY 2 – 5 pm
40% to The Gardens Fund of The National Trust for Scotland
For other opening details see page 133

CULQUOICH, Alford
(Mrs M I Bell Tawse)
Natural woodlands, including an interesting pinetum, shrubs, spring bulbs, azaleas and rhododendrons. Tea and biscuits. Garden is west of Glenkindie village, opposite Glenkindie House, off main Alford-Strathdon road, A97.
Admission £1.00 Children & OAPs 50p
SUNDAY 26th MAY 1.30 – 5 pm
40% to Arthritis and Rheumatism Council

DUNECHT HOUSE GARDENS, Dunecht ♿ (partly)
(Viscount Cowdray)
Romanesque addition, 1877, by G Edmund Street, to original House by John & William Smith. Herbaceous borders, heath and wild garden. Light refreshments. Cars free. Dunecht 1 mile. Routes A974, A944, B 977.
Admission £1.50 Children 50p
SUNDAY 2nd and SUNDAY 9th JUNE 1 – 5 pm
40% to Queen's Nursing Institute (Scotland)
SUNDAY 25th AUGUST 1 – 5 pm
40% to Aberdeen Branch Riding for the Disabled

ESSLEMONT, Ellon ♿
(Mrs Robert Wolrige Gordon of Esslemont)
Victorian house set in wooded policies above River Ythan. Roses and shrubs in garden with double yew hedges (17th and 18th centuries). Music, plant stalls, charity stalls. Home baked teas. Ellon 2 miles. Take A920 from Ellon. On Pitmedden/Oldmeldrum road.
Admission £1.00 Children 50p
SUNDAY 4th AUGUST 1 – 5 pm
25% to Childrens Hospice Association Scotland
15% between Tarves Boys' Brigade and St Mary on the Rock Graveyard.

GLENKINDIE HOUSE, Alford
(Frogmore Investments Ltd)
Policies and garden featuring unusual topiary figures — chess pieces, Alice in Wonderland characters and various 'guardsmen'. Also rose beds, small lake and doocot. Route: A97
Admission £1.00 Children & OAPs 50p
SUNDAY 4th AUGUST 1 – 5 pm
40% to Imperial Cancer Research Fund

HOWEMILL, Craigievar
(Mr D Atkinson)
Young garden with a wide range of unusual alpines, shrubs and herbaceous plants. Plant stall. Teas. From Alford take A980 Alford/Lumphanan road. Suitable for disabled with help. No dogs please.
Admission £1.50 Children under 12 free
SUNDAY 23rd JUNE 1.30 - 5pm
40% to Cancer Relief Macmillan Fund

KILDRUMMY CASTLE GARDENS, Alford   ♿ (with help)
(Kildrummy Garden Trust)
April shows the gold of the lysichitons in the water garden, and the small bulbs
naturalised beside the copy of the 14th century Brig o' Balgownie. Rhododendrons and
azaleas from April (frost permitting). September/October brings colchicums and
brilliant colour with acers, fothergillas and viburnums. Plants for sale. Play area. Video
room. Nature table in spring. Wheelchair facilities. Car park free inside hotel main
entrance. Coach park up hotel delivery entrance. Parties by arrangement.
Tel: 01975 571277/571203. Kildrummy on A97, 10 miles from Alford, 17 miles from
Huntly.
Admission £1.70 Children 6 – 16 50p
Open daily APRIL – OCTOBER
SUNDAY 2nd JUNE 10 am – 5 pm
20% to Queen's Nursing Institute (Scotland) and
20% to Fabric Fund, Kildrummy Church.

#KIRKSTILE HOUSE, Gartly   ♿
(Mr & Mrs R Avis)
Three acre mature garden surrounding 18th century former manse. Many trees, shrubs,
herbaceous borders, walled garden. Teas. Plant stall. No dogs please. 3 miles south of
Huntly off A97 towards Rhynie, or follow Gartly signs from A96.
Admission £1.50 Children free
SUNDAY 14th JULY 2 - 5pm
40% to Action Research for Multiple Sclerosis (Grampian Friends)

LEITH HALL, Kennethmont
(The National Trust for Scotland)
Quadrangular harled mansion dating from 1650. Home of Leith and Leith-Hay family
until 1945. Public rooms contain interesting furniture, personal possessions and
mementoes. The house tour incorporates all of the first floor, including the splendid
oval room and a military collection on second floor. Garden contains a rock garden and
zig-zag herbaceous and catmint borders. Chinese moon gate and Pictish stones.
Extensive grounds with 18th century stables, ponds, including one with a bird
observation hide, three countryside walks with one to a viewpoint overlooking
surrounding countryside. Teas. Pipe band, family games, stalls, competitions. On B9002
near Kennethmont.
Admission £1.60 Children & OAPs £1.00
SUNDAY 21st JULY 1.30 – 5pm
40% to The Gardens Fund of The National Trust for Scotland
For details of other openings see page 130

NETHER AFFLOCH FARMHOUSE, Dunecht   ♿ (with help)
(Mr & Mrs M J Reid)
Interesting 19th century renovated garden with fine views, mature trees, mixed borders,
unusual plants and old fashioned roses, herbs, alpines. Plants for sale. No dogs please.
Route A944.
Admission £2.00 Children £1.00
JUNE to SEPTEMBER, by appointment. Tel. 01330 860362
40% to Ménière's Society

OLD MAYEN, Rothiemay   ♿ (with difficulty)
(Mrs Suki Urquhart)
17th century fortified hall house with 1840 wing. 1½ acre garden started from scratch in 1987. Terraced beds and lawns perched on south facing slope, 200 ft above River Deveron - wonderful views. Walled herb garden, old fashioned shrub roses, mixed shrubs and perennials. Teas. Milltown of Rothiemay 2m, Huntly 10m, Keith 12m. On B9117 between Rothiemay and Marnoch.
Admission £1.50 Children £1.00
SUNDAY 7th JULY 2 - 6pm
40% to Rothiemay Church

OLD SEMEIL HERB GARDEN, Strathdon   (partly)
(Mrs Gillian Cook)
Around 200 varieties of herb plants displayed growing in semi-formal display gardens. Established in 1981 in a sheltered site 1,000 feet above sea level. Specialist nursery, plant sales, tearoom and shop. Extra parking available. Access to patio, tearoom and toilets suitable for wheelchairs. Just off A944 Strathdon/Tomintoul, and 1¼ miles off A97 Huntly/Deeside in Strathdon. Tel: 01975 651343.
Admission by donation. SGS Collection Box.
MAY - AUGUST 10am - 5pm daily
40% to The Henry Doubleday Research Association

PITMEDDEN GARDEN, Ellon ♿
(The National Trust for Scotland)
Garden created by Lord Pitmedden in 1675. Recreated by the Trust from 1952, and is one of the very few gardens of this period in Scotland. Elaborate floral designs in parterres of box edging. Herbaceous borders, yew buttresses, pavilions, fountains and sundials. Also Museum of Farming Life, Visitor Centre, woodland walk. Tearoom. Special rates for pre-booked coach parties.
Admission £3.10 Concessions & children £2.00.
Open daily 1st MAY to 30th SEPTEMBER 10 am – 5.30 pm (Last entry 5 pm)
SUNDAY 14th JULY 1.30 – 5 pm
40% to The Gardens Fund of The National Trust for Scotland
For details of other openings see page 131

STATION COTTAGE, Gartly
(Travers & Betty Cosgrove)
Century old quarry converted into a "secret garden" by generations of railwaymen. Old cottage plants. Climbing pathways through wild garden. Railway site preserved. Teas. Plants for sale. Railway still in use. 5 miles south of Huntly on A97 towards Rhynie. Follow signs for Gartly from A96.
Admission £1.00 Children & OAPs 50p
SUNDAY 30th JUNE 2 - 5pm
40% to Parish of Noth, Church of Scotland

TERTOWIE, Clinterty &

(Aberdeen College)

Half acre walled gardenwith established herbaceous and mixed borders. A new rose garden and seaside garden have recently been added along with new mixed borders. 4 acres of grounds set in mature woodland with shade garden, peat garden & extensive streamside plantings. Many new and unusal varieties of plants as well as the National Collection of Rubus. Woodland walks through surrounding area. Teas. Plant stall. Dogs on lead please. Follow signs for Clinterty from A96 Aberdeen/Inverness, Tertowie signposted at next junction. From A944 Aberdeen/Alford signposted after 5 mile garage.

Admission £1.00 Concessions 50p

SUNDAY 16th JUNE 1 - 4pm

40% to Aberdeen Disabled Persons Trust

TILLYPRONIE, Tarland &

(The Hon Philip Astor)

Late Victorian house. Herbaceous borders, terraced garden with pond at bottom. Shrubs, heaths and ornamental trees in pinetum. Vegetable garden. Superb views. Picnic area. Free car park. Dogs on lead, please. Teas.

Admission £1.00 Children 50p

SUNDAY 25th AUGUST 2 – 5 pm

All proceeds to Scotland's Gardens Scheme

ANGUS

District Organiser: **Mrs Jonathan Stansfeld**, Dunninald, by Montrose DD10 9TD

Area Organisers: **Miss Ruth Dundas,** Caddam, Kinnordy, Kirriemuir DD8 4LP
Mrs R Ephraums, Damside, Leysmill, Arbroath DD11 4RS
Mrs A Houstoun, Kerbet House, Kinnettles, Forfar DD8 1TQ
Mrs R H V Learoyd, Priestoun, Edzell DD9 7UD
Mrs T D Lloyd-Jones, Reswallie House, by Forfar DD8 2SA

Hon. Treasurer: **Col R H B Learoyd,** Priestoun, Edzell DD9 7UD

DATES OF OPENING

House of Pitmuies, Guthrie, by Forfar .... Daily 1 April-31 Oct	10am-5pm
Kinnaird Castle, Brechin .... Sunday 19 May	2 - 5pm
Brechin Castle, Brechin .... Sunday 26 May	2-5.30pm
Kinnettles House, by Forfar .... Sunday 26 May	2 - 6pm
Cortachy Castle, Kirriemuir .... Sunday 2 June	2 - 6pm
Edzell Village & Edzell Castle .... Sunday 16 June	1.30-5.30pm

Reswallie, by Forfar	Sunday 23 June	2-5.30pm
House of Dun, Montrose	Saturday 29 June	12.30-5pm
Newtonmill House, Edzell	Sunday 30 June	2-5.30pm
Barnhill Rock Garden, Broughty Ferry	Saturday 6 July	11am-4pm
Glamis Castle	Sunday 7 July	10.30am-5.30pm
Brechin Castle, Brechin	Sunday 7 July	2-5.30pm
Newtyle Village	Sunday 28 July	1.30 - 5.30pm
Kinpurnie Castle, Newtyle	Sunday 11 August	2 - 6pm

BARNHILL ROCK GARDEN, Broughty Ferry Esplanade &
(Dundee City Council - Leisure & Parks Department)
The Rock Garden has been developed with a geographical theme over 40 years.
In its 5 acres many countries are represented by beds containingtheir native plants.
Attractive water feature. Explanatory leaflet available. Broughty Ferry Gala Week.
Plant stall (1 - 4pm). Teas. Toilets. The garden is close to the Esplanade, one mile east
of Broughty Ferry and south of the A930 Broughty Ferry/Carnoustie road.
Admission by donation
SATURDAY 6th JULY 11am - 4pm
40% to Crossroads

BRECHIN CASTLE, Brechin
(The Earl & Countess of Dalhousie)
Ancient fortress of Scottish kings on cliff overlooking River Southesk. Rebuilt by
Alexander Edward - completed in 1711. Extensive walled garden half a mile from
Castle with ancient and new plantings and mown lawn approach. Rhododendrons,
azaleas, bulbs, interesting trees, wild garden. Tea in garden. Car parking free.
Brechin 1 mile. Route A94.
Admission £1.50 Children 50p
SUNDAY 26th MAY and SUNDAY 7th July 2 - 5.30pm
15% to RSSPC, 15% to Save the Children Fund, 10% to NCCPG

CORTACHY CASTLE, Kirriemuir
(The Earl & Countess of Airlie)
16th century castellated house. Additions in 1872 by David Bryce. Spring garden and
wild pond garden with azaleas, primroses and rhododendrons. Garden of fine
American specie trees and river walk along South Esk. Teas. Garden quiz.
Kirriemuir 5 miles. Route B955.
 Admission £1.75 Children 25p
SUNDAY 2nd JUNE 2 - 6 pm
40% to Royal National Lifeboat Institution

EDZELL VILLAGE & EDZELL CASTLE
Walk round 12 or 13 gardens in Edzell village. Edzell Castle is also on view. Teas extra.
Tickets are on sale in the village and a plan is issued with the tickets. Piper. Plant stall.
Admission £2.00 Children 50p
SUNDAY 16th JUNE 1.30 - 5.30 pm
40% to Crossroads

GLAMIS CASTLE, Glamis ♿
(The Earl & Countess of Strathmore & Kinghorne)
Family home of the Earls of Strathmore and a royal residence since 1372. Childhood home of HM Queen Elizabeth The Queen Mother, birthplace of HRH The Princess Margaret, and legendary setting for Shakespeare's play 'Macbeth'. Five-storey L-shaped tower block dating from 15th century, remodelled 1600, containing magnificent rooms with wide range of historic pictures, furniture, porcelain etc. Spacious grounds with river and woodland paths. Nature trail. Impressive policy timbers. Formal garden. Restaurant. Teas. Four gift shops. Glamis 1 mile A94.
Admission to Castle & grounds: £4.70, OAPs £3.60, children £2.50.
Admission: Grounds only £2.20 Children & OAPs £1.10
SUNDAY 7th JULY 10.30am - 5.30pm
40% to Action Research

HOUSE OF DUN, Montrose ♿
(The National Trust for Scotland)
A fine Georgian house overlooking Montrose Basin, designed and built by William Adam in 1730 for David Erskine, Lord Dun, containing fine furnishing and superb plasterwork by Joseph Enzer. Attractive grounds with magnificent parkland trees and woodland walks. The walled garden has been largely restored to a late Victorian period and includes a range of plants typical of the 1880s. Handloom weavers' workshop. Plant stall. Tearoom. Off A935 4m west of Montrose.
Admission to House & Garden: £3.10 Concessions £2.00 Family Group £8.20.
Garden only £1.00
SATURDAY 29th JUNE 12.30pm - 5pm
40% to The Gardens Fund of The National Trust for Scotland

HOUSE OF PITMUIES, Guthrie, By Forfar
(Mrs Farquhar Ogilvie)
Semi-formal old walled gardens adjoining 18th century house. Massed spring bulbs, roses, herbaceous borders and a wide variety of shrubs. Old fashioned roses in summer with long borders of herbaceous perennials and superb delphiniums. Riverside walk with fine trees, interesting turreted doocot and "Gothic" wash-house. Dogs on lead please. Rare & unusual plants for sale. Fruit in season. Friockheim 1½ m Route A932.
Admission £2.00
Daily 1st APRIL to 31st OCTOBER 10 am - 5 pm
Donation to Scotland's Gardens Scheme

KINNAIRD CASTLE, Brechin ♿
(The Earl & Countess of Southesk)
Small, formal yew garden. Rhododendrons and woodland walks. Deer park. Teas.
Take A933 Arbroath road out of Brechin, follow signs for Kinnaird Park.
Admission £1.50 Children 25p
SUNDAY 19th MAY 2 - 5pm
Donation to St Andrews Church, Brechin

KINNETTLES HOUSE, Douglastown, by Forfar
(Mr & Mrs Hugh Walker-Munro)
Rhododendron walk and rare trees and a mausoleum where an Indian princess is said to be buried. Formal terraced garden. Three miles south of Forfar on A94. Teas. Signed from main road or Dundee/Forfar road, 8 miles. Follow signs for Douglastown.
Admission £1.50 Children free
SUNDAY 26th MAY 2 - 6pm
40% to Kirriemuir Day Centre

KINPURNIE CASTLE, Newtyle
(Sir James Cayzer)
Early 20th century house (not open). Panoramic views of the vale of Strathmore and the Grampians. Shrubs and herbaceous garden. Route B954. Dundee 10 m. Perth 18 m.
Admission £1.50 Children 25p
SUNDAY 11th AUGUST 2 - 6 pm
40% to Angus branch, British Red Cross

NEWTONMILL HOUSE, by Edzell &
(Mr & Mrs Stephen Rickman)
A walled garden comprising of herbaceous borders, rose and peony beds, vegetable beds and doocot. Formal layout with view to house. Donkey rides. Hoopla stall. Plant stall. No dogs please. Teas. B966 Brechin/Edzell road.
Admission £1.75 Children 50p
SUNDAY 30th JUNE 2 - 5.30pm
40% to Scottish Dyslexia Trust

NEWTYLE VILLAGE & (with assistance)
Several cottage gardens, planted in a variety of styles, may be visited in the course of a short walk round the village of Newtyle. The village, with its regular street plan, was laid out in 1832 next to the northern terminus of Scotland's first passenger railway. Tickets and plan on sale at the Village Hall. Plants for sale. Teas in Village Hall. Newtyle is on B954 between Meigle and Dundee, 2 miles off A94 between Coupar Angus and Glamis.
Admission £2.00 including tea Children £1.00, under 5 free
SUNDAY 28th JULY 1.30 - 5.30pm
40% to Chest, Heart & Stroke Scotland

RESWALLIE, by Forfar &
(Col & Mrs T D Lloyd-Jones)
18th century house set in policies of 120 acres. Woodland walks with many interesting trees. Walled herbaceous garden. Vintage cars and motor cycles on display. Plant stall. Teas. Free car parking. Off A932 Forfar/Friockheim. Reswallie signposted to the left.
Admission £1.50 Children 50p
SUNDAY 23rd JUNE 2 - 5.30pm
40% to British Red Cross Society

ARGYLL

District Organiser & Hon Treasurer	**Lt Cmdr H D Campbell-Gibson,** Tighnamara, Melfort, Kilmelford PA34 4XD
Area Organisers:	**Miss Diana Crosland,** Maam, Glen Shira, Inveraray PA32 8XH
	Mrs Charles Gore, Port Namine, Taynuilt PA35 1HU

DATES OF OPENING

Achnacloich, Connel	Daily 1 April-31 October	10am – 6pm
An Cala, Ellenabeich	Daily 1 April-15 October	10am – 6pm
Ardchattan Priory, North Connel.	Daily 1 April-30 October	9am – 9pm

Ardkinglas Woodland Garden .... Open all year
Ardmaddy Castle, Balvicar .... Daily 1 April-31 October or by appt.
Barguillean's 'Angus Garden'Taynuilt .. Open all year
Cnoc-na-Garrie, Ballymeanoch .... 3 Apr,1 May, 5 Jun, 3 Jul, 7 Aug,4 Sep 2-6pm
                                       or by arrangement
Coille Dharaich, Kilmelford .... By appointment
Crarae Glen Garden, Minard .... Daily April-October   9am – 6pm
                                    Winter during daylight hours
Crinan Hotel Garden, Crinan .... Daily 30 April to 30 September
Dalnaheish, Tayvallich .... April-September by appointment
Druimavuic House, Appin .... Daily 14 April-30 June   10am – 6pm
Druimneil House, Port Appin .... Daily 28 March-19 June   9am – 6pm
Eredine Woodland Garden, Lochaweside ... By appointment, Spring-Autumn
Glenfeochan House Hotel, Kilmore .... Daily 15 March-31 October   10am – 6pm
Jura House, Ardfin, Isle of Jura............... Open all year   9am – 5pm
Kildalloig, Campbeltown .... By appointment

Kinlochlaich House Gardens, Appin. ..... Open all year   9.30am – 5.30pm or dusk
                                  (except Sundays Oct-Mar)
Mount Stuart, Rothesay, Isle of Bute ...... 1 May–30 Sep (not Tues & Thurs)
     House: 12–5pm Gardens:11am-5pm. Gardens also open Sat & Sun Apr & Oct
Tighnamara, Kilmelford .... By appointment, Spring – Autumn
Torosay Castle Gardens, ... Open all year
     Isle of Mull .... Summer: 9am-7pm Winter: Sunrise – Sunset

Younger Botanic Garden, Benmore .... Sunday 28 April   10am -6pm
Arduaine, Kilmelford .... Sat&Sun 11/12 May   9.30 – 6pm
Colintraive Gardens Weekend .... Sat&Sun 25/26 May   2 – 6pm
Ardkinglas House, Cairndow .... Sunday 19th May   11am - 6pm
Kyles of Bute Gardens .... Sat&Sun 18/19 May   2 – 6pm
Eredine Woodland Garden, Lochaweside .... Saturdays 25 May & 1 June 11am-6pm
Ardentallen Gardens, Lerags .... Sat&Sun 8/9 June   2 – 6pm
Coille Dharaich, Kilmelford . ... Sat&Sun 15/16 June   2 – 6pm
Tighnamara, Melfort, Kilmelford .... Sat&Sun 15/16 June   2 – 6pm
Ardchattan Priory Fete .... Sunday 21 July
Kildalloig, Campbeltown .... Sunday 28 July   2 - 6pm

ACHNACLOICH, Connel   &

(Mrs T E Nelson)
Scottish baronial house by John Starforth of Glasgow. Succession of bulbs, flowering shrubs, rhododendrons, azaleas and primulas. Woodland garden above Loch Etive. Plants for sale. Admission by collecting box. Dogs on lead please. 3m east of Connel. Admission £1.50   Children free OAPs £1.00
Daily from 1st APRIL to 31st OCTOBER 10am - 6pm
40% between Queen's Nursing Institute (Scotland) and the Gardens Fund of The National Trust for Scotland

AN CALA, Ellenabeich, Isle of Seil
(Mr & Mrs Thomas Downie)
A small garden of under five acres designed in the 1930s, An Cala sits snugly in its horse-shoe shelter of surrounding cliffs. A very pretty garden with streams, waterfall, ponds, many herbaceous plants as well as azaleas, rhododendrons and cherry trees in spring. Proceed south from Oban on Campbeltown road for 8 miles, turn right at Easdale sign, a further 8 miles on B844; garden between school and Inshaig Park Hotel.
Admission £1.00 Children free
Daily from 1st APRIL to 15th OCTOBER 10am - 6pm
Donation to Scotland's Gardens Scheme and Red Cross

ARDCHATTAN PRIORY, North Connel &
(Lt Col R Campbell-Preston)
Beautifully situated on the north side of Loch Etive. The Priory founded in 1230 was the scene of the last Gaelic Parliament. The second oldest inhabited house in Scotland. Formal garden in front of house with two herbaceous, three shrub and a rose border. Wild garden west of house with azaleas, shrub roses, 30 varieties of sorbus and many other shrubs and trees. The front garden leads down to Loch Etive with beautiful views east and west. Tea and light lunches provided daily from 1st April to 30th September. Plant & other stalls. Oban 10m. From north turn left off A828 at Barcaldine (11m south of Appin) on B845 6 miles. From Oban or the east on A85, cross Connel Bridge and turn first right. Proceed east on Bonawe road.
Admission £1.00 Children free
Daily from 1st APRIL to 30th OCTOBER 9am - 9pm.
A fete will be held on **SUNDAY 21st JULY** when the House and Garden will be open.
Donation to Scotland's Gardens Scheme

ARDENTALLEN GARDENS Lerags, by Oban &
ARDENTALLEN HOUSE (Mrs B K Stein)
Small wild garden with rhododendrons, azaleas and heathers.
SONAS (Mr & Mrs C S Motley)
Small garden created in the 1960s from an old quarry. Trees, shrubs, primulas, herbaceous, heathers and rockery. Teas. Home Baking. Dogs on lead please. Take sign to Lerags about one mile south of Oban on A816 until right turn 'Private road to Lower Ardentallen'. Signposted from there.
Admission £1.50 includes both or £1.00 for one garden. Accompanied children free
SATURDAY & SUNDAY 8th & 9th JUNE 2 - 6 pm
20% to Cancer Relief Macmillan Fund
20% to Alzheimer's Society

ARDKINGLAS HOUSE, Cairndow &
(Mr S J Noble)
Set around Ardkinglas House, Robert Lorimer's favourite work, the informal garden of around five acres contains magnificent azaleas, trees and other shrubs. The "Caspian", a large pool, enhances the garden's beauty. Teas, coffee, soft drinks and home baking. Plant stall. Adjacent to Ardkinglas Woodland Gardens. Turn into Cairndow village from A83 Glasgow/Campbeltown road. Enter Ardkinglas estate through iron gates and follow sign.
Admission £1.00 Children free
SUNDAY 19th MAY 11 am - 6 pm
40% to Ardkinglas Arts Trust

ARDKINGLAS WOODLAND GARDEN, Cairndow ♿ (partly)
(Ardkinglas Estate)

This garden contains one of Britain's finest collections of conifers, including "Europe's Mightiest Conifer" and a spectacular display of rhododendrons. Presently, it is undergoing extensive renovation with many improvements already made. It is hoped that visitors will be interested in seeing the garden develop over the coming years. Picnic facilities. Dogs allowed on lead. Entrance through Cairndow village off A83. Admission £1.00

OPEN DAILY ALL YEAR ROUND
Donation to Scotland's Gardens Scheme

ARDMADDY CASTLE, Balvicar, by Oban ♿ (mostly)
(Mr & Mrs Charles Struthers)

Ardmaddy Castle, with its woodlands and walled garden on one side and extended views to the islands and the sea on the other, has some fine rhododendrons and azaleas with a variety of trees, shrubs, unusual vegetables and flower borders betwen box hedges. Woodland walk. Plant stall with some unusual varieties, vegetables when available. Oban 13 miles, Easdale 3 miles. 1½ miles of narrow road off B844 to Easdale. Admission £1.50 Children 50p

Daily 1st APRIL to 31st OCTOBER
Other visits by arrangement: Tel. 01852 300353
Donations to Scotland's Gardens Scheme

ARDUAINE, Kilmelford
(The National Trust for Scotland)

Remarkable coastal garden on a hillside overlooking Loch Melfort and the Sound of Jura. Its internationally famous collection of rhododendron species is mainly sheltered within a Japanese larch woodland while, below, the water garden provides an informal setting for a wide range of trees, shrubs and perennials which thrive in the mild climate of the western seaboard. Located between Oban and Lochgilphead on the A816, sharing an entrance with the Loch Melfort Hotel. Admission £2.10 Children & OAPs £1.40

SATURDAY & SUNDAY 11th & 12th MAY 9.30 am - 6 pm
40% to The Gardens Fund of The National Trust for Scotland
For other opening details see page 122

BARGUILLEAN'S "ANGUS GARDEN", Taynuilt
(Mr Sam Macdonald)

Nine acre woodland garden around eleven acre loch set in the Glen Lonan hills. Spring flowering bulbs, extensive collection of rhododendron hybrids, deciduous azaleas, shrubs, primulas and conifers. Garden recently extended by two acres. Access and car park provided. The garden contains the largest collection of North American rhododendron hybrids in the west of Scotland. Coach tours by arrangement: Tel: 01866 822333 or Fax: 01866 822375. Taynuilt 3 miles.

DAILY ALL YEAR
Donation to Scotland's Gardens Scheme

#CNOC-NA-GARRIE, Ballymeanoch, by Lochgilphead
(Mrs Dorothy Thomson)
A garden being created from rough hillside, designed for year-round interest. Large range of alpines, shrubs, grasses, herbaceous plants and bulbs, many grown from seed. Plant stall. 2m south of Kilmartin, A816. Entrance sharp left between cottages and red brick house, continue up track to bungalow.
Admission £1.00 Accompanied children free.
Wednesdays 3rd APRIL, 1st MAY, 5th JUNE, 3rd JULY, 7th AUG., 4th SEPT. 2 - 6pm
(or by arrangement.) Tel: 01546 605327.
20% to British Red Cross Society (mid Argyll)
20% to Cancer Relief Macmillan Fund

COILLE DHARAICH, Kilmelford, Oban &
(Drs Alan & Hilary Hill)
Small garden, centred on natural rock outcrop, pool and scree terraces and troughs. Wide variety of primulas, alpines, dwarf conifers, bulbs, bog and peat loving plants. No dogs please. Plant stall. Half a mile from Kilmelford on road signposted "Degnish".
Admission £1.00 Children free
SATURDAY & SUNDAY 15th & 16th JUNE 2 - 6 pm
Other days by arrangement. Tel: 01852 200285
40% to North Argyll Eventide Home Association

COLINTRAIVE GARDENS
Two delightful spring and woodland gardens of varied interest, within easy reach of each other. Set in a scenic corner of Argyll.
1 - **Stronailne**   Mr & Mrs H Andrew

2 - **Dunyvaig**   Mrs M Donald

Please call at No. 1 for admission tickets and directions. Dogs on lead please.

Plant stall. On A886, 20 miles from Dunoon.
Admission £1.50 Children 50p includes both gardens
SATURDAY & SUNDAY 25th and 26th MAY 2 - 6 pm
All takings to Scotland's Gardens Scheme

CRARAE, Minard, by Inveraray & (only Lower Gardens)
(Crarae Gardens Charitable Trust)
Rhododendrons, exotic trees and shrubs in a highland glen. Spectacular spring and autumn colour. Dogs on short lead please. Plant sales. Visitor Centre open 10 am - 5 pm April to October. Open winter during daylight hours. Minard 1 mile. Eleven miles south of Inveraray on A83.
Admission: Fixed charge. Car Parking & Children under 5 free
Daily APRIL to OCTOBER 9am - 6pm
Winter during daylight hours
Donation to Scotland's Gardens Scheme

CRINAN HOTEL GARDEN, Crinan
(Mr & Mrs N Ryan)
Rock garden with azaleas and rhododendrons created into the hillside over a century ago and sheltered, secluded garden with sloping lawns, unexpected herbaceous beds and spectacular views of the canal and Crinan Loch. Lochgilphead A83. A816 Oban, then A841 Cairnbaan to Crinan. Donations.
End APRIL to end SEPTEMBER daily
Donation to Scotland's Gardens Scheme

DALNAHEISH, Tayvallich
(Mrs C J Lambie)
Small, informal old garden overlooking the Sound of Jura. Woodland, planted rock, shrubs, bulbs, rhododendrons, azaleas and a wide variety of plants from around the world. Donations. One mile from Tayvallich.
Admission by telephone appointment: Tel. 01546 870286
APRIL to SEPTEMBER
All takings to Scotland's Gardens Scheme

DRUIMAVUIC HOUSE, Appin
(Mr & Mrs Newman Burberry)
Stream, wall and woodland gardens with lovely views over Loch Creran. Spring bulbs, rhododendrons, azaleas, primulas, meconopsis, violas. Dogs on lead please. Plant stall. Route A828 Oban/Fort William, 4 miles south of Appin. Use private road where public signs warn of flooding.
Admission £1.00 Children free
Daily from 14th APRIL to 30th JUNE 10 am - 6 pm
Donation to Scotland's Gardens Scheme

DRUIMNEIL HOUSE, Port Appin
(Mrs J Glaisher)
Ten acre garden overlooking Loch Linnhe with many fine varieties of mature trees and rhododendrons and other woodland shrubs. Home made teas available. Collection box. 2 miles from A828. Connel/Fort William road. Sharp left at Airds Hotel, second house on right.
Admission 50p Children free
Daily from 28th MARCH to 19th JUNE 9am - 6pm
All takings to Scotland's Gardens Scheme

#EREDINE WOODLAND GARDEN, Lochaweside
(Dr & Mrs K Goel)
Woodland garden of 29 acres consisting of attractive mature trees with abundance of wild flowers. Rhododendrons, azaleas, cherry trees and many others. Massed snowdrops followed by daffodils and bluebells. Woodland and lochside walks with spectacular views. Teas - 25th May & 1st June. Dogs on lead please.
On B840. Ford 8m, Dalmally 20m, Inveraray 23m.
Admission £1.00 Accompanied children free.
SATURDAYS 25th MAY and 1st JUNE 11am - 6pm
or by appointment Spring - Autumn. Tel: 01866 844207
40% to Eredine Christian Trust

GLENFEOCHAN HOUSE HOTEL, Kilmore, by Oban
(Mr & Mrs D Baber)
Over 100 different rhododendrons. Azaleas, specimen trees and
tender flowering shrubs. Carpets of spring bulbs and beautiful autumn
colours. Walled garden with herbaceous border, herbs, fruit and vegetables.
Plant stall. Teas. Produce when available. 5 miles south of Oban at head of
Loch Feochan on A816.
Admission £1.50 Children 50p
Daily from 15th MARCH to 31st OCTOBER 10 am - 6 pm
Donation to Scotland's Gardens Scheme

JURA HOUSE, Ardfin, Isle of Jura
(Mr F A Riley-Smith)
Organic walled garden with wide variety of unusual plants and shrubs, including large
Australasian collection. Also interesting woodland and cliff walk, spectacular views.
Points of historical interest, abundant wild life and flowers. Plant stall. Tea tent in
season. Toilet. 5 miles from ferry terminal. Ferries to Islay from Kennacraig by Tarbert.
Admission £2.00 Students £1.00 Children up to 16 free
OPEN ALL YEAR 9 am - 5 pm
Donation to Scotland's Gardens Scheme

#KILDALLOIG, Campbeltown ⅋ (partially)
(Mr & Mrs Joe Turner)
Seaside garden with shrubs, some sub-tropical, and herbaceous perennials. Woodland
walk. Teas. Plant stall. Dogs on lead please. On east coast of Mull of Kintyre, 3m south
of Campbeltown past Davaar island.
Admission £1.00 Accompanied children free.
SUNDAY 28th JULY 2 - 6pm or by appointment. Tel: 01586 553192.
40% to Royal National Lifeboat Institution

KINLOCHLAICH HOUSE GARDENS, Appin ⅋ (Gravel paths sloping)
(Mr D E Hutchison)
Closed Sundays mid October - March. Walled garden, incorporating the West
Highlands' largest Nursery Garden Centre. Display beds of alpines, heathers, primulas,
rhododendrons, azaleas and herbaceous plants. Fruiting and flowering shrubs and
trees. Route A828. Oban 23 miles, Fort William 27 miles. Bus stops at gate by Police
Station.
Admission 70p
OPEN DAILY ALL YEAR 9.30am - 5.30pm or dusk except Sundays October to March..
(Sundays April - Sept. 10.30am - 5.30pm)
40% to Appin Village Hall Fund

KYLES OF BUTE SMALL GARDENS, Tighnabruaich
Three small gardens in and around Tignabruaich within easy reach of each other. Each
garden entirely different with something of interest for everyone. Plant sale. Dogs on
lead please.

1 - **Alt Mhor, Auchenlochan**   Mr & Mrs Peter Scott
2 - **The Cottage**   Col. & Mrs Peter Halliday
3 - **Heatherfield, Kames**   Mr & Mrs David Johnston

Please call at No.1 first for admission tickets and directions.
Admission £1.50 Children 50p includes all 3 gardens
SATURDAY & SUNDAY 18th & 19th MAY 2 - 6 pm
All takings to Scotland's Gardens Scheme

MOUNT STUART HOUSE & GARDENS, Rothesay, Isle of Bute &
(Mount Stuart Trust)
Open to the public for the first time in 1995: ancestral home of the Marquesses of Bute; one of Britain's most spectacular High Victorian Gothic houses, set in 300 acres. Fabulous interiors, art collection and architectural detail; extensive grounds with lovely woodland and shoreline walks; exotic gardens, Victorian kitchen garden; mature Victorian pinetum. Tearoom & picnic areas. Pre-booked house/gardens/ranger guided tours available on application. Admission to House & Garden: £5.50 Child £2.50 Family ticket £15. Concessions and group rates given.
Admission to Garden only: £3 Child £2 Family ticket £8
1st MAY to 30th SEPTEMBER Mon, Wed, Frid, Sat & Sun.
House: 11am - 5pm Gardens: 10am - 5pm (Last admission to both 4.30pm)
Gardens open Saturday & Sunday during April and October.
Donation to Scotland's Gardens Scheme

TIGHNAMARA, Melfort, Kilmelford
(Lt Cmdr & Mrs H D Campbell-Gibson)
Two acre garden set in an ancient oak wood with outstanding views over Loch Melfort. Interesting variety of shrubs and many perennial plants. Paths with terraced beds up hillside. Woodland garden with pool, surrounded by massed primulas, hostas, cranesbill geraniums and astilbes and an abundance of bulbs and wild flowers. Teas. Plant stall. One mile from Kilmelford on lochside road to Degnish.
Amission £1.00 Accompanied children free
SATURDAY & SUNDAY 15th & 16th JUNE 2 - 6pm
By appointment any day between Spring and Autumn. Tel: 01852 200224.
40% to World Society for the Protection of Animals

TOROSAY CASTLE & GARDENS, Isle of Mull
(Mr Christopher James)
Scottish baronial house (1858) by David Bryce. Twelve acre gardens with statue walk attributed to Sir Robert Lorimer c.1899. Craignure 1½ miles. Route: Steamer six times daily from Oban to Craignure. Miniature steam railway from Craignure ferry. Lochaline to Fishnish, then seven miles south on A849. (See full page advertisement).
Admission £2.00 Children & OAPs £1.50
GARDENS OPEN ALL YEAR. Summer 9am-7pm. Winter, sunrise-sunset.
Castle open April to mid-October (extra admission) 10.30am - 5pm
Donation to Scotland's Gardens Scheme

YOUNGER BOTANIC GARDEN & (limited due to hill slopes)
(Specialist Garden of the Royal Botanic Garden, Edinburgh)
World famous for its magnificent conifers and its extensive range of flowering trees and shrubs, including over 250 species of rhododendron. From a spectacular avenue of Giant Redwoods, numerous waymarked walks lead the visitor via a formal garden and pond through hillside woodlands to a dramatic viewpoint overlooking the Eachaig valley and the Holy Loch. Free guided tours of spring colour throughout the open day. James Duncan Cafe (licensed) and Botanics Shop for gifts and plants. Dogs permitted on a short leash. 7m north of Dunoon or 22m south from Glen Kinglass below Rest and Be Thankful pass; on A815.
Admission £2.00 Concessions £1.50 Children 50p Families £4.50
SUNDAY 28th APRIL 10am - 6pm
40% to Royal Botanic Garden, Edinburgh

AYRSHIRE

District Organiser: **The Countess of Lindsey**, Gilmilnscroft, Sorn, Mauchline KA5 6ND

Area Organisers: **Mrs R G Angus,** Ladykirk House, Monkton KA9 2SF
Mrs R F Cuninghame, Caprington Castle, Kilmarnock KN2 9AA
Mrs R Y Henderson, Blairston, by Ayr KA7 4EF
Mrs R M Yeomans, Ashcraig, Skelmorlie PA17 5HB

Hon. Treasurer: **Mr James McFadzean**, Bank of Scotland, 123 High Street, Ayr KA7 1QP

DATES OF OPENING

Blair, Dalry	All year round	
Culzean Castle & Country Park	Daily 1 April–31 Oct	10.30am – 5pm
Culzean Castle & Country Park	Sunday 7 April	10.30am – 5pm
Culzean Castle & Country Park	Sunday 5 May	10.30am – 5pm
Penkill Castle, near Girvan	Sunday 12 May	2 - 5pm
Auchincruive, Ayr	Sunday 19 May	1 – 5.30pm
Kelburn Castle & Country Centre, Fairlie	Wed. 22 May	6 - 8pm
Ashcraig, Skelmorlie	Sunday 26 May	2 - 5.30pm
Doonholm, Ayr	Sunday 2 June	2 – 5.30pm
Barnweil, Craigie, nr Kilmarnock	Sunday 9 June	2 – 5.30pm
Swallow Ha', Symington	Sunday 23 June	2 - 6pm
Culzean Castle & Country Park	Thursday 18 July	10.30am – 5.30pm
Carnell, Hurlford	Sunday 28 July	2 – 5.30pm
Barr Village Gardens	Sat& Sun 3/4 August	1 - 5pm
Skeldon, Dalrymple	Sunday 4 August	2 – 6pm
Blairquhan, Straiton, Maybole	Sunday 11August	1.30 – 4.30pm
Lagg House, Dunure	Sunday 18 August	2 - 5pm

ASHCRAIG, Skelmorlie,
(Mr & Mrs Richard Yeomans)
Garden originally laid out in 1820, presently under renovation, consisting of lawns, woodland and formal gardens, walled garden, also informal cottage garden. Many interesting trees and shrubs including large collection of rhododendrons, azaleas and hydrangeas. Plant stall. Tea and biscuits. Cars free. Skelmorlie approx. 1½ miles north of Largs on A78.
Admission £1.50 Children 50p
SUNDAY 26th MAY 2 - 5.30pm
40% to Cancer Research Campaign (Scotland)

AUCHINCRUIVE, Ayr   ♿
(Scottish Agricultural College)
Classical house of 1764-67 built for the Oswald family. Interior decoration by Robert Adam. Extensive amenity grounds of College campus, the setting for buildings and other facilities serving all aspects of the educational, research and consultancy work of the college. Attractive riverside gardens with plant display, herbaceous and shrub borders; arboretum and a range of outdoor and protected commercial crops at Mansionfield Unit, together forming part of a horticultural teaching & research department. Additional features this year include Farm Walk and Vintage Vehicle Display. Disabled facilities. Car parking free. Afternoon Tea in Oswald Hall. Wide selection of pot plants, shrubs & Auchincruive honey for sale.
Ayr 3m. Route B743. Ayr to Annbank & Tarbolton buses stop at College gate.
Admission £2.50 Children under 14 free OAPs £1.50
SUNDAY 19th MAY 1 - 5.30 pm
40% between Erskine Hospital, the Scottish War Blind and the British Red Cross Society

---

BARNWEIL, Craigie, near Kilmarnock   ♿
(Mr & Mrs Ronald Alexander)
A garden which has been developed from scratch during the last 20 years. Formally planned and colour co-ordinated herbaceous and some shrub rose borders surround the house. These give way to the woodland garden which features rhododendrons, azaleas, ferns, meconopsis and primulas, as well as a golden border. Other features of the garden are beech, and mixed beech and holly hedges, which provide much needed shelter on this rather exposed site. On a clear day, there are fine views to the north for 60-70 miles to Ben Lomond and beyond. Home baked teas. Cars free. Craigie 2 miles.
Route: right off B730, 2 miles south of A77.
Admission £1.50 Children under 12 free
SUNDAY 9th JUNE 2 - 5.30 pm
40% to Tarbolton Parish Church

BARR VILLAGE GARDENS   ♿
A large number of attractive gardens , some old, some new, within this small and beautiful conservation village. Maps and tickets available at each open garden. Teas in Barr Community Hall. Plant stall. Large nursery garden on outskirts of village. Barr is on B734, Girvan 8 miles, Ballantrae 17 miles, Ayr 24 miles.
Admission £1.50 Children under 12 50p
SATURDAY & SUNDAY 3rd & 4th AUGUST 1 - 5pm
40% to Childrens Hospice Association Scotland

BLAIR, Dalry
(Mrs M G Borwick)
Policies open all year round for walkers. Donations welcome.
OPEN ALL YEAR ROUND
All takings to Scotland's Gardens Scheme

BLAIRQUHAN, Straiton, Maybole ♿

(Mr James Hunter Blair)

Castle in Tudor style designed by William Burn, 1820-24. Sixty-foot high saloon with gallery. Lintels and sculptured stones from earlier fortified house incorporated in kitchen courtyard. Original furniture and interesting pictures including gallery with collection of Scottish Colourists. Three mile private drive along the River Girvan. Walled garden with herbaceous border. Regency glasshouse, extensive grounds with specimen trees and views. Admission price includes tour of house. Tea in house. ½ mile west of Straiton. Entry from B7045.

Admission £3.50   Children £2.00   OAPs £2.50

SUNDAY 11th AUGUST 1.30 - 4.30 pm

20% to Ayrshire Hospice   20% to Kyle & Carrick Civic Society

---

CARNELL, Hurlford ♿

(Mr & Mrs J R Findlay)

Alterations in 1843 by William Burn. 16th century peel tower. Walled garden, rock and water gardens; 100 yards herbaceous borders, also vegetables grown with compost. Electrically-heated greenhouses. Flower and plant stalls. Herbaceous borders around Carnell House with plant and home baking stalls. Band. Ice cream and cream teas. Cars free. Kilmarnock 6 miles. Mauchline 4 miles on A76. 1½ miles on Ayr side of A719.

Admission £2.00 Children under 12 free

SUNDAY 28th JULY 2 - 5.30pm

40% to Craigie Parish Church & Craigie Village Hall, KIND, & the British Red Cross Society

---

CULZEAN CASTLE & COUNTRY PARK, Maybole

(The National Trust for Scotland)

Former tower house, castellated and remodelled by Robert Adam 1779-90, complete with viaduct, stables and home farm. Three main garden areas, the Fountain Court (a terraced garden in front of the Castle with an Orangery), the Walled Garden and Herb Garden (herbaceous, semi-tropical trees, shrubs and plants) and Happy Valley (a wild woodland garden with specimen trees and shrubs). Visitor Centre & Restaurant, 18th century castle, deer park, woodland walks, ranger-led excursions, events programme, swan pond and other exhibitions. Route: A719, Maybole 4 miles. Combined ticket for Castle & Country Park: £5.50/£3. Country Park only: £3/£1.50. Additional charge for Castle: £3.50/£1.80. Open 1 Apr-31 Oct 10.30am-5pm.

SUNDAY 7th APRIL, SUNDAY 5th MAY & THURSDAY 18th JULY

Scotland's Garden Scheme Tour 2 - 3.30pm.

40% to The Gardens Fund of The National Trust for Scotland

For other opening details see page 125

DOONHOLM, Ayr   ♿ (limited)

(Mr Peter Kennedy)

Informal gardens in attractive setting on the banks of the River Doon. Mature trees, shrubs and marvellous show of rhododendrons and azaleas. Tea and biscuits. Plant stall. Signposted from Burns Cottage, Alloway and from A77.

Admission £2.00 Children & OAPs £1.00

SUNDAY 2nd JUNE 2 - 5.30pm

40% between Multiple Sclerosis Society and The Samaritans

#KELBURN CASTLE & COUNTRY CENTRE, Fairlie
(The Earl and Countess of Glasgow)
Kelburn Castle dates from the 13th century. The gardens are divided into several areas each having interesting features. Opportunity to visit the recently designed private gardens with emphasis on New Zealand plants. Refreshments. Plant stall. House open - guided tours available, price £1.50 (proceeds to owner). On the A78 between Fairlie and Largs (marked Kelburn Country Centre).
Admission £1.50
WEDNESDAY 22nd MAY 6 - 8pm
40% to Arthritis Care

LAGG HOUSE, Dunure & (mainly)
(Mr & Mrs J Greenall)
Small coastal country garden. Teas. Plant stall. Take A719 coast road from Ayr, three miles from Doonfoot roundabout.
Admission £1.50 Children under 12 free
SUNDAY 18th AUGUST 2 - 5 pm
40% to Action Research (Maybole branch)

#PENKILL CASTLE, near Girvan & (limited)
(Mr & Mrs Patrick Dromgoole)
A series of three Victorian gardens, vegetable, formal and landscaped, linked by a "wild walk" overlooking a burn leading to the Penwhapple river. Currently undergoing restoration work by the present owners. Teas. 3 miles east of Girvan on old Dailly to Barr road.
Admission £1.50
SUNDAY 12th MAY 2 - 5pm
40% to Barr Parish Church

SKELDON, Dalrymple
(Mr S E Brodie QC & Mrs Brodie)
One and a half acres of formal garden and four acres of woodland garden in unique setting on the banks of the River Doon. Large collection of rhododendrons and azaleas, substantial glasshouse collection. Home baked teas. Silver band on the lawn. Plants for sale. Cars free. Dalrymple, B7034 between Dalrymple and Hollybush.
Admission £2.00 Children & OAPs £1.00
SUNDAY 4th AUGUST 2 - 6 pm
40% to the Mental Health Foundation, Kiloran Trust

SWALLOW HA', Symington
(Mr & Mrs Iain Tulloch)
This half acre garden has something of interest around every corner. Bulbs, plants, shrubs and trees ensure year-round colour and variety. Home baked teas. Take B730 west of A77, first left to Symington. Garden 400 yards. No dogs please.
Admission £1.50 Children under 14 free
SUNDAY 23rd JUNE 2 - 6pm
40% to Symington Parish Church

BERWICKSHIRE

District Organiser:	**The Hon Mrs Charles Ramsay,** Bughtrig, Leitholm, Coldstream TD14 4JP
Area Organisers:	**Lt Col S J Furness,** The Garden House, Netherbyres, Eyemouth TD14 5SE
	Miss Jean Thomson, Stable Cottage, Lambden, Greenlaw, Duns TD10 6UN
Hon. Treasurer:	**Mr Richard Melvin,** Bank of Scotland, 88 High Street, Coldstream TD12 4AQ

DATES OF OPENING

Bughtrig, Leitholm .... June–September 11am–5pm, or by appointment
The Hirsel, Coldstream .... Open daily all year, reasonable daylight hours
Manderston, Duns   Sundays & Thursdays 9 May – 29 September

Netherbyres, Eyemouth	Sunday 21 April	2 - 6pm
Manderston, Duns...	Monday 27 May	2-5.30pm
Bughtrig, Leitholm	Sunday 7 July	2.30-5pm
Charterhall, Duns	Sunday 7 July	2 - 5pm
Netherbyres, Eyemouth	Sunday 21 July	2 - 6pm
Manderston, Duns...	Monday 26 August	2-5.30pm

BUGHTRIG, Near Leitholm, Coldstream ♿ (mainly)
(Major General & The Hon Mrs Charles Ramsay)
This is a traditional Scottish family garden, hedged rather than walled and close to the house. It is an interesting combination of herbaceous plants, shrubs, annuals, vegetables and fruit. it is surrounded by fine specimen trees which provide remarkable shelter.   Small picnic area. Parking. Half mile east of Leitholm on B6461.
Admission £1.50   OAPs £1.00   Children under 18 50p
SUNDAY 7th JULY 2.30 - 5pm. Stalls.
20% to The Army Benevolent Fund   20% to SSAFA (Berwickshire branch)
Open daily JUNE to SEPTEMBER 11am-5pm or by appt: 01890 840678
Donation to Scotland's Gardens Scheme

CHARTERHALL, Duns ♿
(Mr & Mrs Alexander Trotter)
Hybrid rhododendrons and azaleas in mature grounds. Flower garden, surrounding modern house. Small greenhouse and vegetable garden. Tea with home bakes and biscuits. Plant stall. 6 miles south west of Duns and 3 miles east of Greenlaw on B6460.
Admission £1.50   Children 50p
SUNDAY 7th JULY 2 - 5 pm
40% to Christ Church, Duns

MANDERSTON, Duns ♿
(The Lord Palmer)
The swan song of the great classical house. Formal and woodland gardens. Tearoom in grounds. 2 miles east of Duns on A6105. Buses from Galashiels and Berwick. Alight at entrance on A6105.
Admission: Prices unavailable at time of going to press.
SUNDAYS & THURSDAYS 9th MAY to 29th SEPTEMBER,
HOLIDAY MONDAYS 27th MAY and 26th AUGUST 2 - 5.30 pm
Parties any time by appointment. Tel: 01361 883450
Donation to Scotland's Gardens Scheme

NETHERBYRES, Eyemouth ♿
(Col S J Furness & GRBS)
Unique 18th century elliptical walled garden, with a new house built inside. Daffodils and wild flowers in the spring. Annuals, roses, herbaceous borders and coloured borders during the summer. Produce stall. Teas in house. Eyemouth quarter mile on A1107.
Admission £1.50   Children 50p
SUNDAY 21st APRIL 2 - 6 pm
40% to British Red Cross Society (Berwickshire branch)
SUNDAY 21st JULY 2 - 6 pm
40% to St Ebba's Church

THE HIRSEL, Coldstream ♿ (mainly)
(The Earl of Home CBE)
Snowdrops and aconites in Spring; daffodils in March/April; rhododendrons and azaleas in late May/early June, and magnificent autumn colouring. Walks round the lake, Dundock Wood and Leet valley. Marvellous old trees. Dogs on leads, please. Homestead Museum, Craft Centre and Workshops. Tearoom (parties please book). Immediately west of Coldstream on A697. Parking charge only.
OPEN DAILY ALL YEAR (Reasonable daylight hours)
Donation to Scotland's Gardens Scheme

CAITHNESS & SUTHERLAND

Joint District Organisers: **Mrs Robert Howden,** The Firs, Langwell, Berriedale, Caithness KW7 6HD

                           Mrs Colin Farley-Sutton, Shepherd's Cottage, Watten, Caithness KW1 5YJ

Area Organiser: **Mrs Richard Tyser,** Gordonbush, Brora KW9 6LX

Hon. Treasurer: **Mr Thom**, Clydesdale Bank plc, 17 Trail Street, Thurso KW14 7EL

DATES OF OPENING

Dunrobin Castle, Golspie	Saturday 22 June	10.30am – 5.30pm
Castle of Mey	Wednesday 17 July	2 – 6pm
Castle of Mey	Thursday 25 July	2 – 6pm
House of Tongue, Tongue	Saturday 27 July	2 – 6pm
Langwell, Berriedale	Sunday 11 August	2 – 6pm
Langwell, Berriedale	Sunday 18 August	2 – 6pm
Castle of Mey	Saturday 7 September	2 – 6pm

CASTLE OF MEY, Mey, Caithness ♿
(H.M. Queen Elizabeth The Queen Mother)
Z-plan castle formerly the seat of the Earls of Caithness. 18th and 19th century additions. Remodelled 1954. Old walled-in garden. On north coast and facing the Pentland Firth and Orkney. Cars free. Teas served under cover. Mey 1½ mile. Route A836. Bus: Please enquire at local bus depots. Special buses can be arranged.
Admission £1.50 Children under 12 £1.00 OAPs £1.00
WEDNESDAY 17th JULY 2 - 6pm
40% to Scottish Disability Foundation (Edinburgh)
THURSDAY 25th JULY and SATURDAY 7th SEPTEMBER 2 - 6pm
40% to Queen's Nursing Institute (Scotland)

HOUSE OF TONGUE, Tongue, Lairg ♿ (partially)
(The Countess of Sutherland)
17th century house on Kyle of Tongue. Walled garden, herbaceous borders, old fasioned roses. Teas available at the Ben Loyal and Tongue Hotels. Tongue half a mile. House just off main road approaching causeway.
Admission to garden £1.50 Children 50p
SATURDAY 27th JULY 2 - 6 pm
40% to the Royal Society for the Prevention of Cruelty to Children

DUNROBIN CASTLE & GARDENS, Golspie
(The Sutherland Trust)
Formal gardens laid out in 1850 by the architect, Barry. Set beneath the fairytale castle of Dunrobin. Tearoom and gift shop in castle. Picnic site and woodland walks. Dunrobin Castle Museum in the gardens. Suitable for disabled by prior arrangement. Group admission: Adults £4.20, children & OAPs £2.50, family £12.50. Castle one mile north of Golspie on A9.
Admission £4.50 Children & OAPs £2.80
SATURDAY 22nd JUNE 10.30 am - 5.30 pm. (Last admission 5 pm)
40% to the British Lung Foundation

LANGWELL, Berriedale &
(The Lady Anne Bentinck)
A beautiful old walled-in garden situated in the secluded Langwell strath. Charming access drive with a chance to see deer. Cars free. Teas served under cover. Berriedale 2 miles. Route A9.
Admission £1.50 Children under 12 £1.00 OAPs £1.00
SUNDAY 11th AUGUST and SUNDAY 18th AUGUST 2 - 6 pm
40% to Royal National Lifeboat Institution

CENTRAL

District Organiser:	**Lady Edmonstone,** Duntreath Castle, Blanefield G83 9AJ
Area Organisers:	**Mrs John Carr,** Duchray Castle, Aberfoyle FK8 3XL
	Mrs Guy Crawford, St Blanes House, Dunblane FK15 0ER
	Mrs Robin Hunt, Keirhill, Balfron G83 0LG
	Mrs John Stein, Southwood, Southfield Crescent, Stirling FK8 2QJ
	Mrs Patrick Stirling-Aird, Old Kippenross, Dunblane FK15 0CQ
	The Hon Mrs R E G Younger, Old Leckie, Gargunnock FK8 3BN
Hon. Treasurer:	**Mrs I M Taylor,** Royal Bank of Scotland, 82 Murray Place, Stirling FK8 2DR

DATES OF OPENING

Daldrishaig House, Aberfoyle .... May to September, by appointment
Kilbryde Castle, Dunblane .... All year, by appointment

Kilbryde Castle, Dunblane	Sunday 17 March	2 – 4pm
Kilbryde Castle, Dunblane	Sunday 14 April	2 – 5pm
West Plean, by Stirling	Sunday 21 April	1.30-4.30pm
The Pass House, Kilmahog	Sunday 28 April	2 – 5.30pm

CENTRAL

Duchray Castle, Aberfoyle	Sunday 5 May	2 - 5pm
Kilbryde Castle, Dunblane	Sunday 5 May	2 – 5pm
Airthrey Estate, Bridge of Allan	Sunday 26 May	2 - 5.30pm
Kilbryde Castle, Dunblane	Sunday 26 May	2 – 5pm
The Pass House, Kilmahog	Sunday 26 May	2 – 5.30pm
Callander Lodge, Callander	Sunday 2 June	2 - 5pm
Old Ballikinrain, Balfron	Sunday 2 June	11am-5pm
Duntreath Castle, Blanefield	Sunday 9 June	2 - 5pm
Kilbryde Castle, Dunblane	Sunday 9 June	2 – 5pm
Daldrishaig House, Aberfoyle	Wednesday 12 June	2 – 5pm
The Blair & Gardens in Blairlogie	Sunday 16 June	2 - 5pm
The Walled Garden, E Lodge, Gean, Alloa	Sunday 23 June	2 - 5pm
Colzium Walled Garden, Kilsyth	Sunday 30 June	2 – 5pm
Kilbryde Castle, Dunblane	Sunday 30 June	2 – 5pm
Bankhead & Park House, Blair Drummond	Sunday 7 July	2 - 5pm
Kilbryde Castle, Dunblane	Sunday 14 July	2 – 5pm
Orchardlea House, Callander	Sunday 28 July	2 - 5pm
Old Ballikinrain, Balfron	Sunday 4 August	2 - 5pm
Kilbryde Castle, Dunblane	Sunday 11 August	2 – 5pm
Kilbryde Castle, Dunblane	Sunday 8 September	2 – 5pm
Kilbryde Castle, Dunblane	Sunday 13 October	2 – 5pm

#AIRTHREY ESTATE, Bridge of Allan ♿
(University of Stirling)
19th century parkland setting laid out by the Thomas Whites in the manner of "Capability" Brown. Since 1967 maintained and developed by the University of Stirling. Set at the southern foot of the Ochil Hills and overlooking the Abbey Craig with the Wallace Monument to the south, the campus is considered to be one of the most beautiful in Europe. Wide range of specimen trees, an arboretum, extensive areas of rhododendrons and other fine shrubs. In the heart of the estate a loch extends to 24 acres attracting a large population of wild fowl. Teas. Plant stall. Off A9 Airthrey road between Stirling and Bridge of Allan or via Hillfoots Road entrance.
Admission £1.50 OAPs £1.00 Children free
SUNDAY 26th MAY 2 - 5.30pm
40% to Local Registered Charities

BANKHEAD & PARK HOUSE, Blair Drummond ♿
(Lady Muir & Richard Muir)
Roses, herbaceous, flowering shrubs. Teas at Bankhead. Cake stall. Tombola. One ticket admits to both gardens. Route: A84. Doune 2m, Stirling 6m.
Admission £1.00 Children 50p
SUNDAY 7th JULY 2 - 5pm
40% to Sight Savers

#CALLANDER LODGE, Leny Feus, Callander
(Miss Caroline Penney)
Romantic Victorian garden. Three acres of mature trees, specimen shrubs, lawns and
herbaceous borders. Waterfall pool and fern grotto. Bog garden. Tea & biscuits. Plant
stall. Route: A84 west through Callander, turn right at sign to Leny Feus. Garden is at
end on left.
Admission £1.50
SUNDAY 2nd JUNE 2 - 5pm
40% to Camphill Village Trust

COLZIUM WALLED GARDEN, Kilsyth &
(North Lanarkshire U.A)
Outstanding collection of conifers and rare trees in beautifully designed walled garden.
No dogs please. Everything well labelled and immaculately maintained. Teas. Plant
stall. On A803 main road through Kilsyth.
Admission £1.00 Children free
SUNDAY 30th JUNE 2 - 5pm
40% to Provost's Local Charities

DALDRISHAIG HOUSE, Aberfoyle
(Mr & Mrs J Blanche)
2½ acre plantsman's garden created in last seven years. Water, scree and herbaceous
gardens. Pottery creatures create a fantasy atmosphere. Tea and biscuits. Garden
pottery stall. Plant stall. Continue straight through Aberfoyle towards Kinlochard for
1½ miles. Very restricted parking, free minibus service from Aberfoyle car park.
Private visits from May to September may be arranged. Tel: 01877 382223.
Admission £1.50 Children free
WEDNESDAY 12th JUNE 2 - 5 pm
40% to Crossroads Care Attendant Scheme
40% to Sight Savers

DUCHRAY CASTLE, Aberfoyle & (with help)
(Mr & Mrs John Carr)
16th century castle, isolated in dramatic countryside overlooking Duchray water.
Formal garden, daffodils, rock garden, lawns, rhododendrons and woodland walks.
Home made teas. Plant and cake stall. Pipe band. 2m west of Aberfoyle through
Queen Elizabeth Forest Park. Free minibus transport available from outside Aberfoyle
Tourist Office.
Admission £2.00 Children & OAPs 50p
SUNDAY 5th MAY 2 - 5pm
40% to Crossroads Care Attendant Scheme

DUNTREATH CASTLE, Blanefield &
(Sir Archibald Edmonstone)
Extensive gardens with mature and new plantings. Landscaped lake, water and bog
gardens. Formal garden, rhododendrons and woodland walk. 15th century keep and
chapel. Pipe band. Dog display. Plant, home cooking and bric-a-brac stalls. Home
made teas. Route: A81 north of Glasgow between Blanefield and Killearn.
Admission £2.00 Children free.
SUNDAY 9th JUNE 2 - 5pm
40% between Greater Glasgow Scouts and Strathard Friends of the Children's Hospice

KILBRYDE CASTLE, Dunblane, Perthshire ♻ (partly)
(Sir Colin & Lady Campbell & Mr J Fletcher)
Traditional Scottish baronial house rebuilt 1877 to replace building dating from 1461.
Partly mature gardens with additions and renovations since 1970. Lawns overlooking
Ardoch Burn with wood and water garden still to be completed. Three miles from
Dunblane and Doune, signposted from both. No teas. No dogs. Children to be
controlled. No toilets. Plants usually for sale.
Admission £2.00 Children under 16 and OAPs £1.50
**SUNDAYS 17th MARCH 2 - 4 pm, 14th APRIL, 5th & 26th MAY, 9th & 30th 14th
JULY, 11th AUGUST, 8th SEPTEMBER, 13th OCTOBER 2 - 5pm.**
Also by appointment. Tel: 01786 823104
*40% to Leighton Library, Strathcarron Hospice, Cancer Relief Macmillan Fund and the Friends of
Dunblane Cathedral*

OLD BALLIKINRAIN, Balfron ♻
(Mrs Caroline Cuthbert)
Specimen trees, shrubberies, woodland walks. Vegetable garden. Herbaceous border.
Plant stall. Teas. Animals to view - ponies, Vietnamese pot bellied pigs, Jacob sheep,
donkeys. 3-D exhibition Women's Royal Voluntary Service on 2nd June. Take A875, turn
off to Fintry B818. House is 1½ miles on.
Admission £2.00 OAPs £1.00 Children & card-carrying WRVS members free
SUNDAY 2nd JUNE 11pm - 5pm
40% to WRVS
SUNDAY 4th AUGUST 2 - 5pm
40% to Camphill Village Trust

ORCHARDLEA HOUSE., Callander ♻
(Mr & Mrs R B Gunkel)
"Secret" garden of about half an acre with a wide variety of trees, shrubs, flowers and
vegetables. Plant stall. Teas on the terrace. Sorry no dogs. Disabled parking only. At
east end of Callander main street (A84). 5 mins. walk from centre of village.
Admission £1.00 Children free
SUNDAY 28th JULY 2 - 5pm
40% to Chest, Heart & Stroke Scotland

THE BLAIR & selected gardens in Blairlogie
Historic village nestling on the south slope of the Ochils. Once renowned for the
recuperative quality of its air and spring waters. The village's open gardens include The
Blair, a small 16th century castle set in terraced gardens overlooking the carse. Mature
magnolias, camellias, rhododendrons and azaleas. Interesting mix of mature and recent
planting. Teas. Half a mile east of the Wallace Monument on A91 near Stirling. Park at
roadside car park, just east of village road.
Admission £1.50 Children free
SUNDAY 16th JUNE 2 - 5pm
40% to Children First

THE PASS HOUSE, Kilmahog, Callander ♿ (partly)
(Dr & Mrs D Carfrae)
Well planted medium sized garden with steep banks down to swift river. Camellias,
rhododendrons, azaleas, alpines and shrubs. Propagating house. Teas. Plant stall.
2 miles from Callander on A84 to Lochearnhead.
Admission £1.00 Children free
SUNDAYS 28th APRIL & 26th MAY 2 - 5.30 pm
40% to Crossroads Care Attendant Scheme

#THE WALLED GARDEN, East Lodge, Gean House, Alloa ♿
(Mr & Mrs A Scott)
One acre Victorian walled garden with original espaliered walks and central arbour.
Mixed herbaceous borders. Large greenhouses. Recreated as faithfully as possible over
the last four years. Woodland walk with decorative implements. Small plant stall.
Take Stirling /Tullibody road straight through Tullibody. 2nd entrance on right after
Jaegar factory.
Admission £1.00
SUNDAY 23rd JUNE 2 - 5pm
40% to The Earl Haig Fund

WEST PLEAN, Denny Road, by Stirling ♿
(Mr & Mrs Graham Johnston)
Walks through a fine display of daffodils in a woodland setting, with walled garden,
duck pond and extensive lawns. Cream Teas. Plant stall. Pony rides. Bric-a-brac stall.
Highland dancers and pipe band. Dogs on leash please. On A872 between Stirling and
Denny just south of Junction 9 M80 & M9.
Admission £1.50 Children 50p
SUNDAY 21st APRIL 1.30 - 4.30pm
40% to Strathcarron Hospice

CLYDESDALE

District Organiser:	**Mrs J S Mackenzie,** The Old Manse, Elsrickle, Lanarkshire ML12 6QZ
Area Organisers:	**Miss A V Mackenzie,** Kippit Farm, Dolphinton, West Linton EH46 7HH
	Mrs M Maxwell Stuart, Baitlaws, Lamington, Lanarkshire ML12 6HR
Hon. Treasurer:	**Mr M J Prime,** Elmsleigh, Broughton Road, Biggar, Lanarkshire ML12 6AM

DATES OF OPENING

#Dippoolbank Cottage, Carnwath	Sunday 16 June	2 - 6pm
Lawhead Croft, Tarbrax	Sunday 16 June	2 - 6pm
Nemphlar Garden Trail, Lanark	Sunday 23 June	2-5.30pm
Stonypath, Dunsyre..	Sunday 30 June	2 - 6pm
Carmichael Mill, Hyndford Bridge	Sunday 7 July	2 – 5pm
Biggar Park, Biggar	Sunday 14 July	2 - 6pm
Dippoolbank Cottage, Carnwath	Sunday 21 July	2 - 6pm
Lawhead Croft, Tarbrax	Sunday 21 July	2 – 6pm
Baitlaws, Lamington, and Glenbreck, Coulter..................................	Sunday 28 July	2 – 6pm
Culter Allers, Coulter	Sunday 4 August	2 – 6pm

BAITLAWS, Lamington, Biggar

(Mr & Mrs M Maxwell Stuart)
The garden has been developed over the past fifteen years with a particular emphasis on colour combinations of hardy shrubs and herbaceous plants, many unusual. Set at around 900 ft above sea level, there are magnificent views of the surrounding hills. Large and varied plant stall. Teas. Route: off A702 above Lamington village. Biggar 5 miles, Abington 5 miles, Lanark 10 miles.
JOINT OPENING WITH GLENBRECK, Coulter.
Admission £1.50 Children over 12 25p
SUNDAY 28th JULY 2 - 6 pm
40% to Biggar Museum Trust

BIGGAR PARK, Biggar & (partially)

(Captain & Mrs David Barnes)
Ten acre garden, starred in the 1996 Good Gardens Guide, incorporating traditional walled garden with long stretches of herbaceous borders and shrubberies as well as fruit, vegetables and greenhouses. Lawns, walks, pools and many other interesting features. Good collection of old fashioned and new specie roses flower in July. Lots of interesting young trees. Home made teas. Plants for sale. ¼ m west of Biggar. Buses from Peebles, Dumfries, Edinburgh etc. stop at front gates. Groups welcome by appointment. Tel: 01899 220185.
Admission £1.75 Children 50p
SUNDAY 14th JULY 2 - 6pm
40% to Multiple Sclerosis Society

CARMICHAEL MILL, Hyndford Bridge, Lanark & (partially)

(Chris & Ken Fawell)
Relatively new garden surrounding workable water mill on River Clyde. Water wheel turning, river level permitting. Semi-formal, informal and wild gardens with fruit and vegetables. Plant stall. A73 Lanark/Biggar road, on left ¼ m from Hyndford Bridge.
Admission £1.50 Children over 12 50p OAPs £1.00
SUNDAY 7th JULY 2 - 5pm
40% to The Lanark Museum Trust

CULTER ALLERS, Coulter ♿ (partially)
(The McCosh Family)
One half of the one acre Victorian kitchen garden is still for the growing of vegetables and fruit while the other half comprises a small lawn, herbaceous borders, a herb garden and a formal rose garden around a well. The remainder of the grounds are open and include a woodland walk and a croquet lawn for those wishing to try their hand. Two or three interesting vehicles on view, weather permitting. Teas. Plant stall. In the village of Coulter, 3 miles south of Biggar on A702.
Admission £1.50 Children free
SUNDAY 4th AUGUST 2 - 6 pm
20% to Coulter Library Trust   20% to Scottish European Aid

#DIPPOOLBANK COTTAGE, Carnwath
(Mr Allan Brash & children)
Artist's intriguing cottage garden. Mainly vegetables grown in small beds. Herbs and fruit, flowers in corners. Route: off B7016 2½ m Carnwath, 3m Auchengray Church Hall. Well signed. JOINT OPENING WITH LAWHEAD CROFT, TARBRAX.
Admission £1.00 Children 20p
SUNDAYS 16th JUNE and 21st JULY 2 - 6pm
40% to Cancer Relief Macmillan Fund

GLENBRECK, Coulter, Biggar
(Hamish Paterson)
Small, mainly herbaceous, garden beside Culter Water in a conservation village.   Teas in Coulter Library until 5pm. Parking at Culter Mill Restaurant. 3 miles west of Biggar on A702.
JOINT OPENING WITH BAITLAWS, Lamington
Admission by collecting box.
SUNDAY 28th JULY 2 - 6 pm
40% to Coulter Library Trust

LAWHEAD CROFT, Tarbrax ♿
(Sue & Hector Riddell)
Cottage, 945 ft above sea level in open Lanarkshire countryside; 1½ acres garden subdivided into enclosures. Some mature, some new with alpine, bonsai, herbaceous, fruit, vegetables and pools, full of surprises - we're plant enthusiasts. Plants for sale. Teas by Auchengray ladies in Auchengray Church Hall, 2½ m towards Carnwath - well signed. Also in Hall, Exhibition of paintings and pottery by local artists.
No dogs please. Route: A70, 12m Balerno, 6m Carnwath and Forth. Signposted from Tarbrax turning. JOINT OPENING WITH DIPPOOLBANK COTTAGE, CARNWATH.
Admission £1.75 Children 20p
SUNDAYS 16th JUNE and 21st JULY 2 - 6 pm
40% to Auchengray & District Charitable Association (Church Hall Central Heating)

NEMPHLAR GARDEN TRAIL, Lanark
Several gardens, medium-sized and small, old and new. Late rhododendrons, primulas, meconopsis, bulbs, flowering shrubs. Teas in Village Hall. Plant stall. Tickets to cover all gardens available at car park or at any of the gardens. 1½ m. north of Lanark off A73.
Admission £1.50
SUNDAY 23rd JUNE 2 - 5.30pm
40% to Children's Hospice Association Scotland

STONYPATH, Little Sparta, Dunsyre, Lanark
(Dr Ian Hamilton Finlay)
"One of the most perceptive of contemporay garden theorists and practitioners" John Dixon Hunt. This neo-classical cottage garden set high in the Pentland Hills has been created over the past 27 years. It contains formal and informal elements including temples and sun dials, woods and pools, a grotto and new features added in the last 2 years. Featured in a 5 page article in the Journal of the Royal Horticultural Society. No dogs please; small children on a lead only (owing to fragile stonework). Paths too narrow for wheelchairs. Signposted from Dolphinton (A702) and Newbigging (A721). Admission £1.50 Children under 12 free
SUNDAY 30th JUNE 2 - 6pm
40% to The Donkey Sanctuary

DUMFRIES

District Organiser:	**Mrs Alison Graham,** Peilton, Moniaive, Thornhill DG3 4HE
Area Organisers:	**Miss E Birkbeck,** Glenstuart, Cummertrees, Annan DG12 5QA
	Mrs Hew Carruthers, Sidings Cottage, Jardine Hall, Lockerbie DG11 1EJ
	Mrs M Johnson-Ferguson, Springkell, Eaglesfield
Hon. Treasurer:	**Mrs S Marchbank,** Chintz & China, East Morton Street, Thornhill DG3 5IX

DATES OF OPENING

Arbigland, Kirkbean	Tuesdays to Sundays: May - September Also Bank Holiday Mondays	2 – 6pm
The Crichton, Dumfries	Sunday 19 May	2 - 5pm
Drumclyer, Irongray	Sunday 26 May	2 - 5pm
Dalswinton House, Auldgirth	Sunday 2 June	2 - 5pm
Craigieburn Garden, Moffat	Sunday 9 June	12.30 – 8pm
Craigielands Mill, Beattock	Sunday 9 June	2 - 5pm
Dalgonar, Dunscore	Sunday 16 June	2 - 5pm
Skairfield, Hightae, Lockerbie	Sunday 30 June	2 - 5pm
Craigieburn Garden, Moffat	Sunday 1 September	12.30 – 8pm

ARBIGLAND, Kirkbean
(Captain & Mrs J B Blackett)
Woodland, formal and water gardens arranged round a secluded bay. The garden where Admiral John Paul Jones worked as a boy in the 18th century. Cars free. Picnic area by sandy beach. Dogs on lead, please. Home baked tea in rustic tea room. Signposted on A710 Solway Coast Road.
Admission £2.00 Children over 5 50p OAPs £1.50
TUESDAYS TO SUNDAYS: MAY - SEPTEMBER 2 - 6 pm.
ALSO BANK HOLIDAY MONDAYS. House open 24th May - 2nd June incl.
Donation to Scotland's Gardens Scheme and SSAFA

CRAIGIEBURN GARDEN, Moffat
(Janet Wheatcroft)
A plantsman's garden specialising in plants of south east Asia. A spectacular gorge and sheltered woodland provide ideal conditions for the National Collection of Meconopsis. Also formal borders, roses, bog garden, peat beds and alpines. Specialist plant nursery. Plants for sale. Parking limited. 2 miles east of Moffat on A708 Selkirk road round bad bends on left, not right.
Admission £1.50 Children free
SUNDAYS 9th JUNE & 1st SEPTEMBER 12.30 - 8pm
40% to the Gurkha Welfare Trust

#CRAIGIELANDS MILL, Beattock &
(Mr & Mrs Michael Henry)
Informal woodland garden created 8 years ago in grounds of converted sawmill. Pond with ornamental ducks. Mill stream. Teas. Sorry no dogs. Route: Off A74 into Beattock village. Follow A701 under railway bridge and immediately right.
Admission £1.50
SUNDAY 9th JUNE 2 - 5pm
40% to Cancer Relief Macmillan Fund

THE CRICHTON, Dumfries
(Crichton Development Company)
Beautiful and extensive grounds of approx. 80 acres containing flowering trees and shrubs, plant centre, rock garden and greenhouses with floral display. The Crichton Memorial Church, an imposing red sandstone building completed in 1897 is located on the site along with many other listed buildings, including Easterbrook Hall. Cars free. Teas at Easterbrook Hall. Route: B725, Dumfries 1 mile.
Admission £1.50 Children 50p
SUNDAY 19th MAY 2 - 5 pm
40% to Crichton Royal Amenity Fund

DALGONAR, Dunscore
(Judge & Mrs William Crawford)
Fine trees, spreading lawns and a traditional wall garden with rose, vegetable and herbaceous borders. Woodland path. Plant stall and teas. First large gates on the right leaving Dunscore for Moniaive.
Admission £1.50 Children 12 and under 50p
SUNDAY 16th JUNE 2 - 5pm
40% to Dunscore Charities

DALSWINTON HOUSE, Auldgirth
(Sir David & Lady Landale)
Woodland and lochside walks. Cake and plant stall. Home baked teas. Dumfries 7 miles. Dumfries/Auldgirth bus via Kirkton stops at lodge.
Admission £1.50
SUNDAY 2nd JUNE 2 - 5pm
40% to Kirkmahoe Parish Church

#DRUMCLYER, Irongray, by Dumfries &
(Mrs Jill Hardy)
Rhododendrons and azaleas. Small woodland garden and walled garden. Teas. Plant stall. Between Shawhead and the Rouken Bridge.
Admission £1.50 Children 50p
SUNDAY 26th MAY 2 - 5pm
40% to Irongray Parish Church

#SKAIRFIELD, Hightae, Lockerbie &
(Mrs M F Jardine Paterson)
Walled garden with herbaceous, fruit and vegetables. Shrubs. Teas under cover. Signed off B7020 between Lochmaben and Dalton.
Admission £2.00 Children £50p OAPs £1.00
SUNDAY 30th JUNE 2 - 5pm
40% to Cancer Research

DUNBARTONSHIRE WEST

District Organiser:	**Mrs W A C Reynolds,** North Stanley Lodge, Cove, Helensburgh G84 0NY
Area Organisers:	**Mrs W J Angus,** Braeriach, 4 Upper Colquhoun Street, Helensburgh G84 9AH
	Mrs James Dykes, Dawn, 42 East Abercromby Street, Helensburgh G84 9JA
	Mrs R C Hughes, Brambletye, Argyll Road, Kilcreggan, G84 0JY
	Mrs J S Lang, Ardchapel, Shandon, Helensburgh G84 8NP
	Mrs E B Ingleby, Denehard, Garelochhead, Helensburgh G84 0EL
Hon. Treasurer:	**Dr D P Braid,** 41 Charlotte Street, Helensburgh G84 7SE

DATES OF OPENING

Auchendarroch, Tarbet .... 1 April-30 June by appt.
Glenarn, Rhu .... Daily 21 March–21 June, sunrise to sunset

Glenarn, Rhu .... Sunday 28 April	2 – 5.30pm
Askival, Kilcreggan .... Sunday 12 May	2 - 5.30pm
Auchendarroch, Tarbet .... Sunday 19 May	2 - 5.30pm
Geilston House, Cardross .... Saturday 25 May	2 – 5.30pm
Ross Priory, Gartocharn .... Sunday 26 May	2 – 6pm
The Linn Garden, Cove .... Sunday 2 June	2 – 6pm
Geilston House, Cardross .... Sunday 14 July	2 – 5.30pm
The Hill House Plant Sale, Helensburgh ...... Sunday 1 September	11am – 5pm

ASKIVAL, Argyll Road, Kilcreggan
(Mr & Mrs D W Geyer)
A largely woodland garden of 1.75 acres, built on a hillside with views to Arran.
Twelve years in the making with over 400 interesting trees and shrubs including
rhododendrons and many different types of eucalyptus and willows. Lily pond, bog
garden and DIY bonsai collection. Teas, baking stall and plant stall. From
Garelochhead on B833, turn right into Argyll Road. Askival is 0.8m along on left.
Admission £1.00 Children 50p
SUNDAY 12th MAY 2 - 5.30pm
40% to S S P C A

AUCHENDARROCH, Tarbet
(Mrs Hannah Stirling)
Five acre garden, superbly set on shores of Loch Lomond. Wild garden, woodland
walk, wide range of heathers, flowering trees and shrubs including cherries,
rhododendrons and azaleas. Regal pelargoniums particularly notable. Plant stall.
Dogs on lead only. Immediately south of Tarbet on A82, lower entrance gate beside
Tarbet Pier.
SUNDAY 19th MAY 2 - 5.30pm
Tea and shortbread. Admission £1.00 Children free
1st APRIL to 30th JUNE by appointment. Tel. 01301 702240
40% to Friends of Loch Lomond

GEILSTON HOUSE, Cardross &
(Miss M E Bell)
L-shaped house of one and two storeys. Additions of about 1830. Walled garden. Glen
with burn. Azaleas, rhododendrons and flowering shrubs. Wild hyacinths. Plant stall.
Sorry no dogs. Cars free. Teas. Cardross 1 mile. Route A814.
Admission £1.50 Children under 12 free
SATURDAY 25th MAY 2 - 5.30 pm
SUNDAY 14th JULY 2 - 5.30pm
All takings to Scotland's Gardens Scheme

GLENARN, Rhu, Dunbartonshire
(Mr & Mrs M Thornley & family)
Woodland garden with burn, daffodils, primulas and bluebells by season, amongst a notable collection of rhododendrons, species and hybrids, as well as magnolias, embothriums and many other fine trees and shrubs. Restoration work in progress at the old pond. Collecting box. Dogs on lead please. No cars up drive. A814 between Helensburgh and Garelochead. Regular bus service, stop at Rhu Marina, up Pier Road to Glenarn Road.
Minimum donation £1.00 Children 50p (Scotland's Gardens Scheme)
DAILY 21st MARCH to 21st JUNE, sunrise - sunset.
Special Opening SUNDAY 28th APRIL 2 - 5.30pm.
Home made teas and plant stall. Admission £1.50 Children 50p.
40% to The Jericho Society

ROSS PRIORY Gartocharn &
(University of Strathclyde)
1812 Gothic addition by James Gillespie Graham to house of 1693 overlooking Loch Lomond. Rhododendrons, azaleas, selected shrubs and trees. Walled garden with glasshouses, alpine beds, pergola, ornamental plantings. Family burial ground. Nature and garden trails. Putting Green. Baking and plant stalls. Tea in house. House not open to view. Cars free. Gartocharn 1½ miles off A811. Bus: Balloch to Gartocharn leaves Balloch at 1 pm and 3 pm.
Admission £1.50 Children free
SUNDAY 26th MAY 2 - 6 pm
20% to Enable
20% to Scottish Down's Syndrome Association

THE HILL HOUSE, Helensburgh & (garden only)
(The National Trust for Scotland)
SCOTLAND'S GARDENS SCHEME PLANT SALE in garden. The Hill House overlooking the estuary of the River Clyde, is considered the finest example of the domestic architecture of Charles Rennie Mackintosh. The gardens are being restored to Walter W Blackie's design with features reflecting the work of Mackintosh.
Admission to Plant Sale free. Donations to SGS welcome
House open separately 1.30 - 5pm. Admission may be restricted.
SUNDAY 1st SEPTEMBER 11 am - 5 pm
40% to The Gardens Fund of the National Trust for Scotland
For other opening details see page 133

THE LINN GARDEN, Cove
(Dr Jim Taggart)
Extensive collections of trees, shrubs, bamboos and water plants surrounding a classical Victorian villa with fine views over the Firth of Clyde. The Linn nursery attached to the garden will be open as usual for the sale of plants and 20% of the afternoon's takings will be donated to Scotland's Gardens Scheme. Teas. Dogs on leads welcome. Entrance 1,100 yards north of Cove village on Shore Road, B833. No parking on Avenue; please park on shore side of main road.
Admission £1.00 Children & OAPs 50p
SUNDAY 2nd JUNE 2 - 6 pm
40% to Shelter (Scotland)

EAST LOTHIAN

District Organiser:	**Mrs D Reid,** North Woodside, Gladsmuir EH33 2AL
Area Organisers:	**Lady Fraser,** Shepherd House, Inveresk, Musselburgh EH21 7TH
	Mrs C Gwyn, The Walled Garden, Tyninghame, Dunbar EH42 1XW
	Mrs M Ward, Stobshiel House, Humbie EH36 5PA
Hon Treasurer:	**Mr R McGee,** Royal Bank of Scotland, 32 Court Street, Haddington EH41 3NS

DATES OF OPENING

Winton House, Pencaitland	Sunday 14 April	2 – 6pm
Tyninghame, Dunbar	Sunday 12 May	2 – 6pm
Lennoxlove, Haddington	Sunday 19 May	12 – 5pm
Stenton Village	Sunday 26 May	2 - 6pm
Dirleton Village	Sat& Sun 1 & 2 June	2 - 6pm
Humbie House, Humbie	Sunday 9 June	2 - 5pm
Stevenson House, nr Haddington	Sunday 16 June	2 – 6pm
Greywalls Hotel, Gullane	Monday 17 June	2 – 5pm
Bowerhouse, Dunbar	Sunday 23 June	2 - 6pm
Greywalls Hotel, Gullane	Monday 24 June	2 – 5pm
Inveresk, near Musselburgh	Sat & Sun 29 & 30 June	2 - 5.30pm
Forbes Lodge, Gifford	Sunday 7 July	2 – 6pm
Greywalls Hotel, Gullane	Monday 8 July	2 – 5pm
Luffness, Aberlady	Sunday 14 July	2 – 6pm
SGS Plant Sale		
Oxenfoord Mains, Dalkeith	Sunday 13 October	11am - 4pm

BOWERHOUSE, Spott, Dunbar ♿ (weather permitting)
(Ian & Moira Marrian)
Bowerhouse is set in 26 acres of garden, orchard and woodland walks. There is an 18th century walled garden which is filled with a wide variety of flowers and shrubs, fruit and vegetables. Within the grounds, you can also find a doocot, wells, a pets graveyard and farmyard animals. Wildlife is attracted by thoughtful planting. The plant stall is being produced by the NCCPG Lothians group and will have many plants not easily available. Home made teas. Route: turn south at the Dunbar A1 bypass sign, Bourhouse/Broomhouse and follow signs for ½ mile.
Admission £1.50 Children 50p OAPs /NCCPG members £1.00 Family ticket £3.50
SUNDAY 23rd JUNE 2 - 6pm
40% to Save the Children Fund

DIRLETON VILLAGE   🧑‍🦽
Small gardens in beautiful village of outstanding architectural interest. Historic kirk.
Teas. Plant stall.
Admission £2.50 includes all gardens. Children 10p
SATURDAY & SUNDAY 1st & 2nd JUNE 2 - 6pm
40% to Dirleton Kirk

FORBES LODGE, Gifford
(Lady Maryoth Hay)
Water garden. Old fashioned shrub roses. Burn. Stalls. Rare plants. Tea.
Admission £1.00
SUNDAY 7th JULY 2 - 6 pm
40% to Children's League of Pity

GREYWALLS HOTEL, Gullane
(Mr & Mrs Giles Weaver)
Six acres of formal garden attributed to Gertrude Jekyll complements the Edwardian
house built by Sir Edward Lutyens in 1901. Rose garden, herbaceous, shrub and annual
borders.
Admission £1.50 Accompanied children free
MONDAYS 17th & 24th JUNE & 8th JULY 2 - 5pm
All takings to Scotland's Gardens Scheme

HUMBIE HOUSE, Humbie   🧑‍🦽
(Mr & Mrs Robert Laing)
Herbaceous borders, vegetable and fruit gardens, old rose garden, shrubs and trees in
10 acres. From A68 take Humbie turning at Fala B6368, 1m east of Humbie.
Admission £1.50 Children 50p
SUNDAY 9th JUNE 2 - 5pm
40% to Cancer Research and Wellbeing

INVERESK, near Musselburgh

Catherine Lodge	-	Mr Philip Mackenzie Ross
Eskhill House	–	Robin & Lindsay Burley (Sunday only)
Inveresk Lodge	-	The National Trust for Scotland
Manor House	-	Mr & Mrs Harry More-Gordon
Oak Lodge	-	Mr & Mrs Michael Kennedy
Rose Court	-	Mr & Mrs George Burnet
Shepherd House	-	Sir Charles & Lady Fraser

Inveresk is a unique and unspoiled village on the southern fringes of Musselburgh.
There have been settlements here since Roman times. The present houses mostly date
from the late 17th and early 18th century. All have well laid out gardens enclosed by
high stone walls. Each garden has its own individual character - some formal, some
less so, some old, some new. They all contain a wide range of shrubs, trees and many
interesting and unusual plants. Plant stall. Teas on Sunday only.
Admission £3.00 OAPs £2.50 (includes all gardens) Accompanied children under 12 free
SATURDAY & SUNDAY 29th & 30th JUNE 2 - 5.30pm
40% to Arthritis Care

LENNOXLOVE, Haddington   ♿ (partly)
(The Duke of Hamilton)
Lennoxlove, parts of which date back to the 14th century, houses the core of the famous Hamilton Palace collection of pictures, porcelain and furniture, also the death mask, casket and ring of Mary, Queen of Scots. The lime avenue, known as Politician's Walk, is where Secretary Maitland pondered the affairs of state during Queen Mary's reign. 17th century sundial by Gifford. The ancient keep is approached by way of a roundel of wild cherry trees containing a 40ft star of snowdrops, in the centre of which is an ash planted by Queen Elizabeth, the Queen Mother in 1967. The white Cadzow herd of wild cattle may be seen across the ha-ha. Plant stall. Tea room open: 12 - 5pm. Guided tours of house every 30 minutes 12 - 5pm. Route: 1½ m south of Haddington on B6369, 18m east of Edinburgh off A1.
Admission £1.00 Children 20p Guided tour of house £2.00
SUNDAY 19th MAY 12am - 5 pm
40% to the Lennoxlove Trust

LUFFNESS, Aberlady   ♿ (weather permitting)
(Luffness Limited)
16th century castle with earlier foundations. Fruit garden built by Napoleonic prisoners-of-war. Tea in house. Plant stall. Donations please.
SUNDAY 14th JULY 2 - 6 pm
40% to Scottish Society for the Prevention of Cruelty to Animals

STENTON VILLAGE GARDENS   ♿ (some)
Stenton is a conservation village considered to be the best preserved in East Lothian. Several varied and interesting gardens in and around the village will be open. Teas and maps available in the Village Hall. Plant stall. A festival of flowers in Stenton Parish Church. Follow signs from A1 East Linton/Dunbar.
Admission £2.00 to all include all gardens.   Children over 14 and OAPs £1.00
SUNDAY 26th MAY 2 - 6pm
40% to Alzheimer's Scotland

STEVENSON HOUSE, near Haddington   ♿
(Mrs J C H Dunlop)
House garden includes wide lawns surrounded by large flowerbeds containing a mixture of herbaceous plants and shrubs, a rose garden, spring border and rock edge. Woods and dell containing many fine trees. Walled kitchen garden undergoing a programme of replanting; many unusual plants in new beds, linked by a collection of *Betula* species. Some good specimen trees, with interesting underplantings. Herbaceous central walk, extensive vegetable beds, fruit. Plant stall of garden-reared cuttings. Outwith gardens, a circular walk takes in new riverside tree belt and continues through poplar wood, being replanted with trees for future coppicing. Stevenson House marked on A1 between Haddington & East Linton. Historic House signs on A1 and on road from Haddington.
Admission to grounds, including parking £2.00
SUNDAY 16th JUNE 2 - 6 pm
20% to Malcolm Sargent Cancer Fund for Children   20% to Epilepsy Association of Scotland

TYNINGHAME, Dunbar ♿
(Tyninghame Gardens Ltd)
Splendid 17th century pink sandstone Scottish baronial house, remodelled in 1829 by William Burn, rises out of a sea of plants. Herbaceous border, formal rose garden, Lady Haddington's secret garden with old fashioned roses, formal walled garden with sculpture and yew hedges. The 'wilderness' spring garden with magnificent rhododendrons, azaleas, flowering trees and bulbs. Grounds include one mile beech avenue to sea, famous 'apple walk', Romanesque ruin of St Baldred's Church, views across parkland to Tyne estuary and Lammermuir Hills. Tyninghame 1 mile.
Admission £1.50 Children 75p
SUNDAY 12th MAY 2 - 6 pm
40% to Abbeyfield East Linton Society Ltd

WINTON HOUSE, Pencaitland
(Sir David Ogilvy's 1968 Trust)
17th century Renaissance house. Decorative stone chimneys and dormers. William Wallace, master mason. Early 19th century castellated entrance. Beautiful plaster ceilings and stone carving, fine pictures and furniture. Masses of daffodils. Fine trees, terraced gardens. House conducted tour: £3.50, children under 14 £1.00. Tea and biscuits in house. From Pencaitland, lodge and wrought-iron gates two thirds of a mile on A6093, or, on B6355, archway and wrought-iron gates one mile from New Winton village, drive half a mile.
Admission £1.00 Children 25p
SUNDAY 14th APRIL 2 - 6 pm
40% to Royal Commonwealth Society for the Blind

SGS PLANT SALE
A Bring and Buy Plant Sale will be held at Oxenfoord Mains, Dalkeith on
SUNDAY 13th OCTOBER 11am - 4pm.
Route: 4 miles south of Dalkeith on A68, turn left for one mile on A6093.
Admission free.

EDINBURGH & WEST LOTHIAN

Joint District Organisers: **Mrs J C Monteith,** 7 West Stanhope Place, Edinburgh EH12 5HQ

Mrs Charles Welwood, Kirknewton House, Kirknewton, West Lothian EH27 8DA

Joint Hon. Treasurers: **Mrs J C Monteith and Mrs Charles Welwood**

DATES OF OPENING

Newliston, Kirkliston .... Wednesdays to Sundays inclusive
1 May – 2 June   2 – 6pm

CAMBO HOUSE, KINGSBARNS, Fife
(Mr & Mrs T. P. N. Erskine)
Snowdrop Day – Sunday, 25th February, 2-5 p.m. (provisionally)
Sunday, 12th May, 2-5 p.m.   Open all year round 10-5p.m.

Photograph by Brian Chapple

BOLFRACKS, ABERFELDY, Perth & Kinross
(Mr J. D. HUTCHISON, CBE)
Daily 1st April to 31st October, 10-6 p.m.

Photograph by Brian Chapple

CLUNY HOUSE, ABERFELDY, Perth & Kinross
(Mr J. & Mrs W. Mattingley)
Daily 1st March to 31st October, 10-6 p.m.

Photograph by Brian Chapple

DRUMMOND CASTLE GARDENS, CRIEFF, Perth & Kinross
(Grimsthorpe & Drummond Castle Trust Ltd)

Sunday, 4th August, 2–6 p.m.   Open Daily May to October 2–6 p.m. (last entrance 5 p.m.)

Photograph by Brian Chapple

HOUSE OF PITMUIES, GUTHRIE, BY FORFAR, Angus
(Mrs Farquhar Ogilvie)
Daily 1st April to 31st October, 10–5 p.m.

Photograph by Brian Chapple

LATHRISK HOUSE & OLD LATHRISK, FREUCHIE, Fife
(Mr & Mrs David Skinner and Mr & Mrs David Wood)
Sunday 21st July, 2-5.30 p.m.

Photograph by Moira Leggat

PREPARING FOR THE SGS PLANT SALE AT HILL OF TARVIT, CUPAR, Fife
Saturday 5th October, 10.30–4 p.m. and Sunday 6th October, 2-5 p.m.

Photograph by Moira Leggat

TIGHNAMARA,
MELFORT, KILMELFORD,
Argyll
(Lt Cmdr & Mrs H. D. Campbell
Gibson)
Saturday & Sunday,
15th & 16th June, 2–6 p.m.
and by appointment Spring
& Autumn

Photograph by Brian Chapple

COILLE DHARAICH,
KILMELFORD, Argyll
(Drs Alan & Hilary Hill)
Saturday & Sunday,
15th & 16th June, 2–6 p.m.
and by appointment

Photograph by Brian Chapple

EDZELL VILLAGE & EDZELL CASTLE, Angus
Sunday 16th June, 1.30–5.30 p.m.

Photograph by Brian Chapple

Dalmeny Park, South Queensferry	Date to be announced	
The Trefoil Centre, Gogarbank	Saturday 13 April	2 – 5pm
Dean Gardens & Ann Street, Edinburgh	Sunday 14 April	2 – 6pm
Foxhall, Kirkliston	Sunday 21 April	2 – 5.30pm
Redhall Walled Garden, Edinburgh.....................	Saturday 27 April	10am-3pm
Hethersett, Balerno..	Sunday 28 April	2-5.30pm
Dr Neil's Garden, Duddingston	Sat & Sun 11/12 May	2 – 5pm
Colinton Gardens, Edinburgh	Sunday 19 May	2 – 5pm
Arthur Lodge, Dalkeith Road, Edinburgh...........	Sat & Sun 15/16 June	2 – 5pm
Kirknewton House, Kirknewton	Sun-Fri 16 -21 June	2-6pm
Mill Lade House, Edinburgh	Sunday 16 June	2-5.30pm
Malleny House Garden, Balerno..........................	Wednesday 26 June	2 – 5pm
Redhall Walled Garden, Edinburgh.....................	Wednesday 26 June	10am-3pm
Swanston Gardens	Sat & Sun 29/30 June	2 - 5pm
Belgrave Crescent Gardens, Edinburgh...............	Sunday 21 July	2 – 5pm
Suntrap Horticultural Centre, Edinburgh	Sunday 4 August	2 – 5pm
Dr Neil's Garden, Duddingston	Sat & Sun 10/11 August	2 – 5pm
South Queensferry & Dalmeny	Sunday 11 August	1 – 6pm
SGS Plant Sale, Kirknewton House.....................	Saturday 28 September	11 - 4pm
	& Sunday 29 September	2 - 5pm

ARTHUR LODGE, 60 Dalkeith Road, Edinburgh &
(Mr S R Friden)
Formal herbaceous garden. Sunken Italian garden and White garden. Plant stall. Teas.
Entrance to garden in Blacket Place, opposite the Commonwealth Pool.
Admission £1.50 Children £1.00
SATURDAY & SUNDAY 15th & 16th JUNE 2 - 5pm
40% to Cockburn Association (Pinkerton Fund)

BELGRAVE CRESCENT GARDENS, Edinburgh &
(Belgrave Crescent Proprietors)
Central city garden with lawns and trees, shrubs and flowers and paths leading down
to the Water of Leith and a waterfall. Refreshments available. Route: first left over
Dean Bridge out of Edinburgh.
Admission £1.00 Children & Senior Citizens 50p
SUNDAY 21st JULY 2 - 5 pm
40% to St Columba's Hospice, Edinburgh

COLINTON GARDENS, Edinburgh
MILLHOLME, Grant Avenue (Mr Cecil Mcgregor)
Rhododendrons, shrubs and rock garden. From village, proceed up Woodhall Road,
second left turn, then first right (Grant Avenue) entrance on right. Refreshments.
MOUNT PLEASANT, 5 Castlelaw Road (Mr William Alexander)
Spring flowering shrubs, rhododendrons, camellias. Car park free. Tea and biscuits.
Mount Pleasant is 70 yards up Castlelaw Road.
Admission to each garden £1.00 Children under 8 free
SUNDAY 19th MAY 2 - 5 pm
Millholme: 40% to The Order of St Lazarus Charitable Fund
Mount Pleasant: 40% to Scotland's Gardens Scheme

DALMENY PARK, South Queensferry
(The Earl of Rosebery)
Acres of snowdrops on Mons Hill. Cars free. Teas will be available in the Courtyard
Tearoom, Dalmeny House. Route: South Queensferry, off A90 road to B924.
Pedestrians and cars enter by Leuchold Gate and exit by Chapel Gate.
Admission £1.50 Children under 14 free
DATE TO BE ANNOUNCED
40% to St Columba's Hospice

DEAN GARDENS & ANN STREET, Edinburgh
DEAN GARDENS (Dean Gardens Committee of Management)
Privately owned town gardens on north bank of the Water of Leith. 13½ acres of
spring bulbs, daffodils, trees and shrubs and other interesting features. Entrance at Ann
Streeet or Eton Terrace.
ANN STREET GARDENS
Ann Street is one of the few Georgian streets where the houses on both sides boast their
own front gardens. They are particularly pretty in spring and early summer with
flowering trees, shrubs and bulbs.
Admission to both gardens £1.00 Children 50p
SUNDAY 14th APRIL 2 - 6 pm
All takings to Scotland's Gardens Scheme

DR NEIL'S GARDEN, Duddingston Village
(Drs Andrew & Nancy Neil)
Landscaped garden on the lower slopes of Arthur's Seat using conifers, heathers and
alpines. Teas in Kirk Hall. Plant stalls. Car park on Duddingston Road West.
Admission £1.25 Children free
SATURDAY & SUNDAY 11th & 12th MAY 2 - 5 pm
SATURDAY & SUNDAY 10th & 11th AUGUST 2 - 5 pm
All takings to Scotland's Gardens Scheme

FOXHALL, Kirkliston
(Mr & Mrs James Gammell)
Daffodils and woodland walk. Plant stall. Cake stall. Turn east at lights in centre of
Kirkliston, half mile on right, sign at road end, Conifox Nursery.
Admission £2.00 Children under 14 free OAPs £1.00
SUNDAY 21st APRIL 2 - 5.30 pm
40% to St Columba's Hospice

HETHERSETT, Balerno
(Professor & Mrs I G Stewart)
Informal, woodland garden with daffodils, primulas and rhododendrons.
No dogs please. Plant stall. Route: On A70, half mile beyond Balerno turning.
Parking at Ravelrig.
Admission £1.50 Children 50p
SUNDAY 28th APRIL 2 - 5.30pm
20% to Barnardo's   20% to Riding for the Disabled

KIRKNEWTON HOUSE, Kirknewton &

(Mr & Mrs Charles Welwood)

Extensive woodland garden. Rhododendrons, azaleas and shrubs. Plant stall. No dogs please. Route: Either A71 or A70 on to B7031.

Admission £2.00 Children under 14 free

SUNDAY 16th to FRIDAY 21st JUNE 2 - 6 pm

(Teas on Sunday weather permitting)

40% to St Columba's Hospice

SGS Bring & Buy PLANT SALE

Saturday 28th SEPTEMBER 11am - 4pm & Sunday 29th SEPTEMBER 2 - 5pm

---

MALLENY HOUSE GARDEN, Balerno &

(The National Trust for Scotland)

A two acre walled garden with 17th century clipped yew trees, lawns and borders. Wide and varied selection of herbaceous plants and shrubs. Shrub roses including NCCPG. 19th century rose collection. Ornamental vegetable and herb garden. Greenhouse display. Scottish National Bonsai Collection. Plant stall. Tea and biscuits. In Balerno, off Lanark Road West (A70) 7m from Edinburgh city centre. Buses: Lothian 43, Eastern Scottish, 66 & 44.

Admission £1.00 Children & OAPs 50p

WEDNESDAY 26th JUNE 2 - 5 pm

40% to The Gardens Fund of The National Trust for Scotland

For other opening details see page 133

#MILL LADE HOUSE, 13 Belford Place, Edinburgh

(Mr & Mrs Guy Severn)

Hillside garden of 1½ acres in the centre of Edinburgh. Shrubs, ground cover and water garden. Teas. Plant stall. The garden is on lower level beyond Edinburgh Sports Club where parking is available. No 13 bus route along Belford Road.

Admission £1.50 Children free

SUNDAY 16th JUNE 2 - 5.30pm

40% to Home Link

NEWLISTON, Kirkliston &

(Mr J S Findlay)

18th century designed landscape. Rhododendrons and azaleas. The house, which was designed by Robert Adam, is open and a collection of costumes will be on display. Teas. On Sundays tea is in the Edinburgh Cookery School which operates in the William Adam Coach House. Also on Sundays there is a ride-on steam model railway from 2 - 5 pm. Four miles from Forth Road Bridge, entrance off B800.

Admission to House & Garden £1 Children & OAPs 50p

WEDNESDAYS - SUNDAYS inclusive each week from1st MAY to 2nd JUNE 2 - 6pm

40% to King George V Fund for Sailors

#REDHALL WALLED GARDEN, 97 Lanark Road, Edinburgh &

(Scottish Association for Mental Health)

A traditional walled garden built in the 18th century. Now a listed garden it is run on organic principles as a mental health project. Teas. Plant stall.

Admission 50p Children free

SATURDAY 27th APRIL and WEDNESDAY 26th JUNE 10am - 3pm

40% to Scottish Association for Mental Health

SOUTH QUEENSFERRY & DALMENY

Around twelve small gardens in varied styles - cottage, water, plantsman's, bedding. Teas. Tickets and maps available from Dalmeny Kirk Hall and Queensferry Parish Church, The Loan.

Inclusive admission £1.50 Accompanied children free OAPs £1.00

SUNDAY 11th AUGUST 1 - 6 pm

40% to RNLI, South Queensferry

SUNTRAP HORTICULTURAL & GARDENING CENTRE 43 Gogarbank, Edinburgh &

(Oatridge Agricultural College, organised by Friends of Suntrap)

A horticultural out-centre of Oatridge Agricultural College. Compact garden of 1.7 hectares (3 acres), includes rock and water features, sunken garden, raised beds, woodland plantings & greenhouses. Facilities for professional and amateur instruction, horticultural advice and a place to visit. Refreshments. Plant sales. Gardening advice. Parking for disabled drivers inside main gate, other car parking opposite. Signposted 0.5m west of Gogar roundabout, off A8 and 0.25m west of Calder Junction (City bypass) off A71. Bus route: Lothian Transit 37. Open daily throughout the year 9am - 4.30 pm. Friends of Suntrap in garden at weekends April to September 2.30 - 4.30pm. Admission £1.00 Children & OAPs 50p

SUNDAY 4th AUGUST 2 - 5pm

40% to The National Trust for Scotland (Broughton House Garden)

#SWANSTON OLD FARMHOUSE & GARDENS AT SWANSTON VILLAGE

800 ft above sea level. Traditional gardens and thatched cottages. The summer haunt of Robert Louis Stevenson. Teas. Plant stall. Home baking stall. Close to city bypass at the end of Swanston Road.

Admission £1.50 OAPs £1.00 includes all gardens.   Children free

SATURDAY & SUNDAY 29th & 30th JUNE 2 - 5pm

40% to The Thistle Foundation

THE TREFOIL CENTRE, Gogarbank &

Daffodils, woodland walk and grounds all suitable and accessible for disabled people. Admission price includes tea or coffee. Home baking. Souvenir shop. Children's play area. Ratho 2 miles, Edinburgh 6 miles. From A8 Gogar roundabout, first left, past Gogarburn, ½ mile over railway bridge, sharp right and ½ mile past Suntrap. Admission £2.00 Children £1.00 OAPs £1.00

SATURDAY 13th APRIL 2 - 5 pm

40% to Trefoil Centre, Holidays for the Disabled

ETTRICK & LAUDERDALE

District Organiser: **Mrs Gavin Younger,** Chapel-on-Leader, Earlston TD4 6AW

Hon. Treasurer: **Mr L Haldane,** Royal Bank of Scotland, St Dunstan's
High Street, Melrose TD6 9PF

DATES OF OPENING

Bemersyde, Melrose .... Sunday 21 April		2 – 6pm
The Old Manse, Legerwood .... Friday 5 July		6 - 8.30pm
Chapel-on-Leader, Earlston .... Sunday 7 July		2 - 6pm
Mellerstain, Gordon .... Sunday 14 July		12.30 – 6.30pm
Abbotsford, Melrose .... Sunday 4 August		2 – 5.30pm

ABBOTSFORD, Melrose   ♿ (partly)
(Mrs P Maxwell-Scott, OBE)
House and garden built and laid out by Sir Walter Scott, who built the house 1812-1832
when he died. Herbaceous and annual borders. Teashop in grounds. Jedburgh Branch
Royal British Legion Pipe Band. Admission to house and garden: £3.00, children £1.50.
Bus party - adults £2.20, children £1.10. Melrose 2 miles, Galashiels 1½ miles.
Admission to garden only: £2.00
SUNDAY 4th AUGUST 2 - 5.30 pm
40% to The Thistle Foundation

BEMERSYDE, Melrose   ♿
(The Earl Haig)
16th century peel tower reconstructed in the 17th century with added mansion house.
Garden laid out by Field Marshal Earl Haig. Views of Eildon Hills. Woodland walks.
Admission to garden only. St Boswells via Clintmains or Melrose via Leaderfoot Bridge.
Admission £1.65 Children under 10 free
SUNDAY 21st APRIL 2 - 6 pm
40% to Lady Haig's Poppy Factory

CHAPEL-ON-LEADER, Earlston   ♿
(Mr & Mrs Gavin Younger)
Large country garden with lovely views of park and river. Inspired by Sissinghurst and
Jekyll, planting is informal with interesting foliage as well as flowers. Divided into
different areas there is a white garden, rose avenue, azalea border, mixed borders with
old fashioned roses, clematis and rose covered pergolas, paved swimming pool area,
recently restored water and bog garden, woodland and rhododendron walks and a
large walled kitchen garden. Home made teas. Turn off A68 at sign 2m north of
Earlston, 4m south of Lauder.
Admission £2.00 Children free
SUNDAY 7th JULY 2 - 6pm
40% to Save the Children Fund

MELLERSTAIN, Gordon   ♿
(The Earl of Haddington)
Adam mansion with formal terrace and rose garden. Extensive grounds with lake and many fine trees. Tearoom in grounds. House open 12.30 - 5 pm; last admission 4.30 pm. Admission to House and Garden: £4.00, OAPs £3.00, Children £1.50. Route: Gordon, 3 miles on A6089 or at turn off A6105 from A68 at Earlston 6 miles, both signposted Mellerstain House.
Admission to garden only: £1.50
SUNDAY 14th JULY 12.30 - 6.30 pm
Donation to Scotland's Gardens Scheme

#THE OLD MANSE, Legerwood, by Earlston
(Mr & Mrs Meyrick Ovens)
18th century manse adjoining church of 1127 with Norman arch. Shrub roses, many interesting shrubs and herbaceous borders. Views to the Cheviots. Plant stall. Wine. Turn off A68 2½ m north of Earlston, 4m south of Lauder, signed Legerwood. Admission £5.00 including wine. Children free
FRIDAY 5th JULY 6 - 8.30pm
40% to Legerwood Church

FIFE

District Organiser:	**Mrs David L Skinner**, Lathrisk House, Freuchie KY15 7HX
Area Organisers:	**Mrs James Barr,** Burnbank, Drumhead, Saline KY12 9LL
	Mrs Christine Gordon, The Tannery, Kilconquhar, Leven KY9 1LQ
	Mrs Roderick F Jones, Nether Kinneddar, Saline KY12 9LJ
	Mrs N Stewart-Meiklejohn, 6 Howard Place, St Andrews KY16 9HL
	Mrs Robert Turcan, Lindores House, Cupar KY14 6JD
Hon. Treasurer:	**Mrs A B Cran,** Karbet, Freuchie KY15 7EY

DATES OF OPENING

Cambo House, Kingsbarns	Daily all year 10am – 5pm	
Micklegarth, Aberdour	20 May - 31 August by appointment	
Cambo House, Kingsbarns	Sunday 25 February (provisionally)	2 – 5pm
Barham, Bow of Fife	Sunday 28 April	12 - 4pm
Cambo House, Kingsbarns	Sunday 12 May	2 – 5pm
Saline Village gardens	Sunday 12 May	2 – 6pm
Micklegarth, Aberdour	Sunday 19 May	2 – 5pm

Whitehill, Aberdour	Sunday 26 May	2 – 5.30pm
Falkland Palace Garden	Sunday 2 June	2 – 5pm
Gilston, Largoward	Sunday 9 June	1.30 – 6pm
Culross Palace Garden	Sunday 16 June	11am – 5pm
Myres Castle, Auchtermuchty	Sunday 16 June	2 – 5pm
Balcaskie, Pittenweem	Sunday 23 June	2 – 6pm
Hill of Tarvit, Cupar	Sunday 23 June	12.30 – 5pm
Barham, Bow of Fife	Sat & Sun 29/30 June	2 – 5.30pm
46 South Street, St Andrews	Sunday 30 June	11.30 – 5.30pm
St Andrews Botanic Garden	Sunday 30 June	10am – 6pm
Hilton House, Cupar	Sunday 7 July	2.30 – 5pm
Kellie Castle, Pittenweem	Sunday 7 July	1.30 – 5pm
Balcarres, Colinsburgh	Sunday 14 July	2 – 5pm
Crail Gardens	Sat & Sun 20/21 July	2 – 6pm
Lathrisk & Old Lathrisk, Freuchie	Sunday 21 July	2 – 5.30pm
Falkland Palace Garden	Sunday 4 August	1.30 – 5pm
Pittenweem Gardens	Sat & Sun 10/11 August	2 – 5.30pm
Hill of Tarvit Plant Sale	Saturday 5 October	10.30am – 4pm
	Sunday 6 October	2 – 5pm

#46 SOUTH STREET, St ANDREWS &
(Mrs Alan Baxter)
Access from Greenside Place only.
On original "long rigg" including an 18th century doocot with a garden room, an old
pear avenue, mature trees and recently planted shrub roses, shrubs and plants.
Tea and coffee. Plant stall. Greenside Place is parallel to South Street and can be
reached from Abbey Street or Queens Gardens.
Admission £1.50 Children 50p
SUNDAY 30th JUNE 11.30 - 5.30pm
40% to Reels for Romania

BALCARRES, Colinsburgh &
(The Earl & Countess of Crawford & Balcarres)
19th century formal and woodland garden; wide variety of plants. Teas. Plant stall.
½ mile north of Colinsburgh off A921.
Admission £2.00 Accompanied children free
SUNDAY 14th JULY   2 - 5 pm
20% to Colinsburgh SWRI   20% to Colinsburgh Town Hall

BALCASKIE, Pittenweem ♿ (top terrace only)
(Sir Ralph Anstruther of that Ilk Bt.)
There has been a house, originally fortified, at Balcaskie since the 13th century and a
charter granted to Ivor Cook by King Alexander III in 1223 exists. In 1665 Sir William
Bruce altered the castle, laid out the terraces and made what he called " the first
mansion house in Scotland". He lived there before building, and moving to, Kinross
house. The Anstruther family acquired the property in 1698. Tea and biscuits. National
Trust and SSAFA stalls. East Neuk Pipe Band. Route: A917, 2 miles from Anstruther.
Enter by Lodge gate.
Admission £2.00 Children free
SUNDAY 23rd JUNE 2 - 6 pm
40% to SSAFA

BARHAM, Bow of Fife ♿
(Sir Robert & Lady Spencer Nairn)
A garden full of character and friends. Herbaceous borders and island beds with
shrubs and old fashioned roses. Also a vegetable garden and a woodland garden in the
making with rhododendrons, shrubs, spring bulbs and ferns. Plant stall. Teas.
Route: A91 4 miles west of Cupar. No dogs please.
Admission £1.50 Children under 12 free
SUNDAY 28th APRIL 12 - 4pm Plant Stall. Hot soup and rolls.
40% to International Spinal Research Trusts
SATURDAY & SUNDAY 29th & 30th JUNE 2 - 5.30pm
40% to Pain Association Scotland

CAMBO HOUSE, Kingsbarns ♿
(Mr & Mrs T P N Erskine)
A romantic garden designed around the Cambo burn. It is a traditional walled garden
serving the superb Victorian mansion house (not open) with flowers, fruit and
vegetables. The garden retains many original features with greenhouses and clipped
box hedges. A woodland walk along the burn leads to the beach. Many rare and
unusual plants. The season starts early with acres of snowdrops and snowflakes.
Massed daffodils and spring bulbs follow. Over 220 named roses. Chrysanthemums
and a colchicum meadow give autumn colour. Plant stall. Cars free. Dogs on lead
please. Route: A917.
Admission £2.00 Children free
OPEN ALL YEAR ROUND 10 am - 5 pm
SNOWDROP DAY - Provisionally SUNDAY 25th FEBRUARY 2 - 5 pm
40% to Arthritis & Rheumatism Council
SPRING OPENING - SUNDAY 12th MAY 2 - 5 pm
40% to British Diabetic Association

CRAIL: SMALL GARDENS IN THE BURGH
(The Gardeners of Crail)
A number of small gardens in varied styles: cottage, historic, plantsman's, bedding.
Exhibition of paintings at Lobster Cottage, Shoregate. Approach Crail from either St
Andrews or Anstruther, A917. Park in the Marketgate. Tickets and map available only
from Mrs Auchinleck, 2 Castle Street, Crail.
Admission £2.00 Acccompanied Children free OAPs £1.00
SATURDAY & SUNDAY 20th and 21st JULY 2 - 6 pm
20% to Children's Hospice Association Scotland   *20% to Crail Preservation Society*

FIFE

CULROSS PALACE GARDEN, Culross
(The National Trust for Scotland)
Built between 1597 and 1611, the house was not a Royal Palace, but the home of Sir George Bruce, a rich merchant. It features painted ceilings and has recently been restored and furnished. A model 17th century garden was created at the same time as the house restoration, and reflects what a successful merchant of the period might have grown to support his household - vegetables, culinary and medicinal herbs, soft fruit and flowering meads. Terraced and on a steep slope, it is laid out mainly in raised beds. Sections are partitioned by willow hurdle fences, and the path surface is made up of crushed shells.
Admission to Palace, garden, Town House and Study £3.60, concessions £2.40
Admission to garden £1.00 Children & OAPs 50p
SUNDAY 16th JUNE 11am - 5pm
40% to The Gardens Fund of the National Trust for Scotland
For other opening details see page 126

FALKLAND PALACE GARDEN, Falkland &
(The National Trust for Scotland)
The Palace was the hunting seat of the Stewart monarchs during the 15th and 16th centuries. The present garden was laid out after the last war by Percy Cane on the site of the original Royal Garden and contains a Royal Tennis Court built in 1539 and in play today. Tearooms nearby in village. Free car park. Route: A912.
Admission to Palace and garden £4.10, concessions £2.70.
Admission to Garden £2.00 Children £1.00
SUNDAY 2nd JUNE and SUNDAY 4th AUGUST 1.30 - 5 pm
40% to The Gardens Fund of the National Trust for Scotland
For other opening details see page 126

GILSTON, Largoward
(Mr Edward Baxter)
Late 18th century house with informal and wild gardens, primulas, meconopsis, rhododendrons and azaleas. Herbaceous and shrub borders. Wildflower meadow and butterflies. National Trust for Scotland and plant stalls. Teas. 8 miles from St Andrews, 6 miles from Leven on A915.
Admission £2.00 Accompanied children free
SUNDAY 9th JUNE   1.30 - 6 pm
40% to The Game Conservancy

HILL OF TARVIT, Cupar
(The National Trust for Scotland)
Charming Edwardian mansion house designed in 1906 by Sir Robert Lorimer for jute magnate, Mr F B Sharp. Contains his fine collection of furniture, paintings, tapestries and Chinese porcelain. The house stands in beautiful grounds with many interesting and unusual plants, shrubs and trees. Heathers and heaths, rose garden and delightful woodland walk to toposcope. Perfect place for a picnic. Tea room. Plant stall.
Route A916. Admission to house and garden: £3.10, concesssions £2.00
Admission to garden: £1.00 Children & OAPs 50p
SUNDAY 23rd JUNE 12.30 - 5 pm
40% to The Gardens Fund of The National Trust for Scotland
For other opening details see page 127

73

FIFE

SCOTLAND'S GARDENS SCHEME PLANT SALE, Hill of Tarvit
Bring plants, buy plants. Large variety of shrubs and big clumps of herbaceous plants at bargain prices.
Saturday - Coffee & snack lunches.   Sunday - Teas.
SATURDAY 5th OCTOBER 10.30am-4pm   SUNDAY 6th OCTOBER 2 - 5pm
40% to East Fife Members Centre of The National Trust for Scotland

---

HILTON HOUSE, Cupar
(Mrs M M Wilson)
Walled garden, roses and herbaceous. Hill garden walk. Garden stall. Cream teas. One mile north of Cupar passing Adamson Hospital.
Admission £1.50 Children under 12 free
SUNDAY 7th JULY 2.30 - 5pm
40% between Cupar Society for the Blind, Childrens Hospice Association Scotland and St James' Church, Cupar

---

KELLIE CASTLE, Pittenweem &
(The National Trust for Scotland)
The oldest part of the castle dates from about 1360. The building, mainly 16th and 17th century probably assumed its present dimensions about 1606. Kellie is a very fine example of the domestic architecture of lowland Scotland. Virtually abandoned in the early 19th century, the castle was leased to, and restored by, Professor James Lorimer from 1876. Includes Lorimer exhibition and children's nursery Walled organic garden features box edged paths, rose arches, herbaceous plants and shrub roses.
Admission to house and garden £3.10, concessions £2.00. Tearoom within castle available to those visiting garden only. Good picnic area.
Admission to Garden £1.00 Children & OAPs 50p
SUNDAY 7th JULY 1.30 - 5 pm
40% to The Gardens Fund of the National Trust for Scotland
For further opening details see page 129

LATHRISK HOUSE & OLD LATHRISK, Freuchie &
(Mr & Mrs David Skinner and Mr & Mrs David Wood)
Herbaceous borders, shrubs, lawns and mature trees in beautiful setting with views over the Howe of Fife and East Lomond. Teas. Cake and produce stall. Plant stall.
Admission £1.50 Children free
SUNDAY 21st JULY 2 - 5.30pm
40% to Falkland Parish Church

MICKLEGARTH, Aberdour
(Gordon & Kathleen Maxwell)
Small, informal garden with shrubbery, herbaceous and island beds and rock garden. Teas. Plant & produce stall. In heart of historic seaside village. Route: A921. Train, bus or car to Aberdour, park in car park at railway station; proceed west along High Street approximately 200 metres.
Admission £1.50 Accompanied children free OAPs £1.00
SUNDAY 19th MAY 2 - 5 pm
40% to Save the Children Fund
Thereafter to 31st AUGUST by appointment. Tel: 01383 860796
20% to Aberdour Scout Group   20% to Local Registered Charities

MYRES CASTLE, Auchtermuchty   ♿
(Captain David Fairlie)
Fortified house, with 18th century additions, built in 1530 by John Scrymgeour, Master of the King's Works, who completed Falkland Palace for James V in 1542. Woodland gardens with pond. Layout of walled garden based on one of the Vatican gardens. Yew hedges form 'garden rooms' for flowering shrubs. Beds of shrub, hybrid roses and herbaceous plants and lupins. Plant stall. Home baked teas under cover. A chance to meet the Scouts in camp. Cars free. ¼ m south of Auchtermuchty on A983 to Falkland. Perth/Kirkcaldy buses stop at Myres Castle Lodge. 100 yards walk to garden.
Admission £2.00   Children free OAPs £1.00
SUNDAY 16th JUNE   2 - 5pm
40% to Cupar District Scouts

PITTENWEEM: SMALL GARDENS IN THE BURGH
(The Gardeners of Pittenweem)
A good number of small gardens in varied styles, hidden in the streets and wynds of this beautiful and rather secretive burgh. Two excellent tea rooms in High Street. Many exhibitions of contemporary art running concurrently with garden openings. Festival in village starts 7th August. Nice dogs welcome. Tickets and map available only from Mrs M G Williamson, Priorsgait, 15 Cove Wynd. Route: A917.
Admission £2.00 Accompanied children free OAPs £1.00
SATURDAY & SUNDAY 10th & 11th AUGUST 2 - 5.30 pm
40% between The Anthony Nolan Bone Marrow Trust & Pittenweem Festival

---

SALINE VILLAGE GARDENS
A number of small and large gardens. Saline is five miles north-west of Dunfermline. Gardens will be signposted. No dogs please. Teas will be provided in Village Hall. Route: Junction 4 M90 and then on to B194. Cars can be parked in centre of village near bus stop, where maps and tickets will be sold.
Admission £2.00 Accompanied children free OAPs £1.00
SUNDAY 12th MAY 2 - 6 pm
40% between Driving for the Disabled, The National Asthma Campaign & Saline Church Heating Fund

---

ST ANDREWS BOTANIC GARDEN, Canongate, St Andrews   ♿
(Fife Council)
Peat, rock and water gardens. Tree, shrub, bulb and herbaceous borders. Large range of plants. Plant stall. Route: A915. Well signposted in St Andrews.
Admission £1.00 Accompanied children 50p
SUNDAY 30th JUNE 10 am - 6 pm
40% to Friends of the Botanic Garden

WHITEHILL, Aberdour   ♿
(Mr & Mrs Gavin Reed)
Shrubs and specie rhododendrons, a fine collection of interesting trees and a new lochan. Teas. Good plant stall. Route: B9157.
Admission £1.50
SUNDAY 26th MAY 2 - 5.30pm
40% to Royal Blind Asylum & School

GLASGOW & DISTRICT

District Organiser:	**Mrs J Thomson,** Hexagon House, Bardowie Loch G62 6EY
Area Organisers:	**Mrs C M T Donaldson,** 2 Edgehill Road, Bearsden G61 3AD
	Mrs F T Crossling, 28 North Grange Rd, Bearsden G61 3AF
	Mrs P Oldfield, Bystone Mews, East Kilbride Road, Clarkston G76 8RU
Hon. Treasurer:	**Mr M Smith,** 60 Cleveden Drive, Kelvinside G12 0NX

DATES OF OPENING

Invermay, Cambuslang .... April - September by appt.		
Calderglen Country Park .... Sunday 31 March	5.30-8pm
Greenbank Garden &		
Greenbank House, Clarkston .... Sunday 14 April	11am – 5pm
60 Cleveden Drive, Kelvinside.............................. Sunday 12 May	2 – 5pm
Acre Valley House, Torrance .... Sunday 2 June	2 – 5pm
Kittoch Mill, Carmunnock .... Sunday 23 June	2 – 5pm
Whitemoss House, East Kilbride .... Sunday 23 June	2 – 5pm
Bystone Mews, Busby.. Sunday 7 July	2 – 5pm
Six Fathoms, Eaglesham .... Sunday 4 August	2 - 5pm
Glasgow Botanic Garden .... Sunday 11 August	12-4.45pm

60 CLEVEDEN DRIVE, Kelvinside ♿ (partly)
(Matthew Smith)
A plant person's communal garden with a little of everything - alpines, herbaceous, heathers and conifers, herbs, wildflowers, vegetables and small wildlife ponds all in a compact garden shared by nine flats. Good plant stall, with many unusual. Off Great Western Road, approx. half mile from the Botanics. Numerous buses, e.g. 66.
Admission £1.00 Children over 12 50p
SUNDAY 12th MAY 2 – 5pm
40% to NCCPG (Strathclyde)

#ACRE VALLEY HOUSE, Torrance ♿ (limited)
(Mr & Mrs Glen Collins)
A two acre garden being recently restored with varied planting of hardy shrubs and herbaceous plants and some beautiful mature trees. No dogs please.
Teas. Plant stall. Route: B822 Torrance/Lennoxtown. In centre of Torrance turn into West Balgrochan Road and, at end of speed limit, right into Acre Valley Road.
Admission £1.00 Children over 12 50p
SUNDAY 2nd JUNE 2 - 5pm
40% to Driving for the Disabled (Fintry group)

BYSTONE MEWS, Clarkston
(Mr & Mrs G C Oldfield)
One acre garden created by present owners in 1987 from neglected wasteground originally forming part of boundary of Bystone Estate. Now well established with wishing well, mini woodland walk, bulbs, herbaceous and a good variety of conifers and shrubs, all providing year round interest. Plant stall. On A726 East Kilbride/Busby. Police permission has been granted to park on nearside lane of dual carriageway. Additional parking at Railway Inn, Busby (7 mins. walk)
Admission £1.00 Children free
SUNDAY 7th JULY 2 - 5pm
40% to Imperial Cancer Research

#CALDERGLEN COUNTRY PARK: Conservatory & Gardens, East Kilbride &
(East Kilbride District Council)
Guided tours of the new conservatory containing a collection of world wide flora and fauna natural to their continents of origin. Also the enclosed garden featuring a parterre, shrub borders, alpine beds, large pond, aviaries with owls, coati-mundis and farmyard exhibits. Refreshments. Plant stall. Follow signs for Strathaven A726. Admission by donation to Scotland's Gardens Scheme.
SUNDAY 31st MARCH 5.30 - 8pm
All takings to Scotland's Gardens Scheme

#GLASGOW BOTANIC GARDENS
(Glasgow City Council)
Visit the Propagation Houses and the internationally renowned Filmy Fern House, not normally open to the public. The main house was built in 1878 and the principal specialist named collections are of orchids, begonias and ferns. Teas. Corner of Queen Margaret Drive & Great Western Road. Leave motorway at Junction 17, follow signs for A82 Dumbarton.
Admission: Suggested donation £1.00 Children 50p
SUNDAY 11th AUGUST 12 - 4.45pm
All takings to Scotland's Gardens Scheme

GREENBANK HOUSE & GARDEN, Clarkston &
(The National Trust for Scotland)
Daffodil Day: visitors can see over 200 named varieties of daffodil in the walled demonstration garden, and many other older varieties naturalized in the surrounding woodland. Guided walks with the Gardening Instructor, Mr Jim May.
Greenbank House will contain a display of named daffodils and an exhibition on Scotland's Gardens Scheme. Springtime floral demonstrations by the Scottish Association of Floral Arrangement Societies will be staged at 2pm and 3pm (admission £1). Raffle. Plant stall. Teas by the Friends of Greenbank. Clarkston 1mile. Bus: Strathclyde no.44D to Mearnskirk or Newton Mearns; alight at Flenders Road. Admission to Garden £2.60 Children & OAPs £1.70.
SUNDAY 14th APRIL 11am - 5pm
40% to The Gardens Fund of The National Trust for Scotland
For other opening details see page 133

INVERMAY, 48 Wellshot Drive, Cambuslang
(Mrs M Robertson)

A plant lovers' garden. Wide variety of unusual bulbs, rock plants, herbaceous plants, shrubs (many named) in a very sheltered, suburban garden. Greenhouse with fuchsias. Something in flower all through the year - a special town garden. Teas. Plant Stall. A730 (East Kilbride) or A749/A724 (Hamilton) from Glasgow. Convenient to M74/M73. Wellshot Drive starts at back of Cambuslang station.
Admission £1.50 Children over 12 50p
APRIL to SEPTEMBER by appointment. Tel. 0141 641 1632
40% to Children First

KITTOCH MILL, Carmunnock
(Brigadier & Mrs Howard Jordan)

This waterside and woodland garden contains the National Collection of Hostas in Scotland with over 300 varieties growing in different conditions. Many varieties and species of ligularia are planted out on the river banks and woodland areas. A new Japanese-style garden has been created close to the house featuring a Yatsu-Hashi (zig-zag bridge) which leads the visitor to the woodland area. Many other unusual plants are to be seen and the garden is a haven for native flora and fauna. Plant stall with many gems from the garden. Please - no dogs. Situated off B759 Busby/Carmunnock. Parking is allowed on far side of road.
Admission £1.00
SUNDAY 23rd JUNE 2 - 5pm
40% to N C C P G (Strathclyde)

SIX FATHOMS, 6 Polnoon Street, Eaglesham &
(Mr & Mrs A Bewick)

A really useful garden with a little of everything - flowers, fruit, vegetables and a pond. Plant stall. B767 Glasgow/Eaglesham. B764 East Kilbride/Eaglesham.
Admission £1.00 Children over 12 50p
SUNDAY 4th AUGUST 2 - 5pm
40% to Eastpark Home for Children

WHITEMOSS HOUSE, East Kilbride
(Mr & Mrs Albert Heasman)

An open plan garden of about one acre, developed over the past 20 years. Contains a variety of acid loving shrubs and perennials, mostly grown from seed or cuttings. Teas. Plant stall. In Whitemoss Recreation Area opposite bowling greens and tennis courts. Enter via the John Wright Sports Centre car park, Calderwood Road and follow signs.
Admission £1.00 Children over 12 50p
SUNDAY 23rd JUNE 2 - 5pm
40% to East Kilbride & District Hospice Care Appeal

ISLE OF ARRAN

District Organiser: **Mrs S C Gibbs,** Dougarie, Isle of Arran KA27 8EB

Hon. Treasurer: **Mr J Hill,** Bank of Scotland, Brodick, Isle of Arran KA27 8AL

DATES OF OPENING

Dougarie .... Sunday 30 June	2 - 5pm
Brodick Castle & Country Park .... Wednesday 10 July	10am – 5pm
Brodick Castle & Country Park .... Wednesday 7 August	10am – 5pm

BRODICK CASTLE & COUNTRY PARK ♿ (mostly)
(The National Trust for Scotland)
Semi-tropical plants and shrubs. Walled garden. Rock garden. Free guided walks. Car park free. Morning coffee, lunch and tea available in Castle. NTS shop. Brodick 2 miles. Service buses from Brodick Pier to Castle. Regular sailings from Ardrossan and from Claonaig (Argyll). Information from Caledonian MacBrayne, Gourock. Tel: 01475 33755.
Admission to Garden & Country Park £2.10. Children & OAPs £1.40
WEDNESDAYS 10th JULY and 7th AUGUST 10 am - 5 pm
40% to The Gardens Fund of the National Trust for Scotland
For other opening details see page 123

DOUGARIE
(Mr & Mrs S C Gibbs)
Terraced garden in castellated folly. Shrubs, herbaceous borders, traditional kitchen garden. Tea. Produce stall. Blackwaterfoot 5 miles. Regular ferry sailing from Ardrossan and from Claonaig (Argyll). Information from Caledonian MacBrayne, Gourock. Tel: 01475 337355.
Admission £1.00 Children 50p
SUNDAY 30th JUNE 2 - 5pm
40% to Arran Cancer Support

KINCARDINE & DEESIDE

District Organiser: **Mrs J Mackie,** Bent, Laurencekirk AB30 1EA

Area Organisers: **The Hon Mrs J K O Arbuthnott,** Kilternan, Arbuthnott, Laurencekirk AB30 1NA

Mrs E H Hartwell, Burnigill, Burnside, Fettercairn AB30 1XX

Dr Frances McCance, House of Strachan, Strachan Banchory AB31 3NN

Hon. Treasurer: **Mr D S Gauld,** 18 Reed Crescent, Laurencekirk AB30 1EF

DATES OF OPENING

Shooting Greens, Strachan .... 28 April – 12 May by arrangement

Shooting Greens, Strachan	Sunday 28 April	2 – 5pm
Inchmarlo House Garden, Banchory	Sunday 26 May	1.30-5pm
Crathes Castle, Banchory	Sunday 23 June	2 – 5pm
Drum Castle, Drumoak	Sunday 7 July	1.30 – 5pm
Glassel Lodge, Banchory	Sunday 14 July	2 - 5pm
House of Strachan, Banchory	Sunday 21 July	2 - 5pm
Balmanno, Marykirk	Sunday 28 July	2 – 5.30pm
Douneside House, Tarland	Sunday 28 July	2 – 5pm
Glenbervie House, Drumlithie	Sunday 28 July	2 – 5pm

BALMANNO, Marykirk, by Laurencekirk   ♿ (gravel paths)
(Mr & Mrs Ronald Simson)
A traditional Scottish 18th century walled garden with flower borders and vegetable plots. Splendid views of the Grampians. Home baked teas. Plant stall. Balmanno is three-quarters of a mile north of Marykirk. Turn right at unmarked crossroads, up hill a few hundred yards on right.
Admission £1.50 Children 50p
SUNDAY 28th JULY 2 - 5.30 pm
20% to Macmillan Cancer Ward, Stracathro Hospital
20% to Marykirk Hall Rebuilding Fund

CRATHES CASTLE, Banchory &

(The National Trust for Scotland)

Richly decorated tower house of the north eastern school built by the family of Burnett of Leys between 1553-96. Good examples of painted ceilings, fine furniture and interesting portraits. Walled gardens (3.75 acres) containing eight distinct and separate gardens, including magnificent yew hedges planted in 1702, rare shrubs and fine herbaceous borders. All combine to form the finest patterned garden in northern Scotland. Extensive wild gardens and grounds containing adventure playground, picnic areas and some 10 miles of marked trails. Exhibitions, shop and licensed restaurant. Sale of plants, garden walks, ranger walks. Situated off A93, 3 miles east of Banchory.

Admission quoted includes castle, garden, estate and use of all facilities.

Admission (combined ticket) £4.10 Children & OAPs £2.70

SUNDAY 23rd JUNE   2 - 5 pm

40% to The Gardens Fund of The National Trust for Scotland

For other opening details see page 124

DOUNESIDE HOUSE, Tarland &

(The MacRobert Trust)

Ornamental and rose gardens around a large lawn with uninterrupted views to the Deeside Hills and Grampians; large, well-stocked vegetable garden, beech walks and water gardens. Cars free. Tea in house. Plant stall. Ballater and District Pipe Band. Tarland 1½ miles. Route: B9119 towards Aberdeen.

Admission £1.50 Children & OAPs £1.00

SUNDAY 28th JULY 2 - 5 pm

40% to Gardeners' Royal Benevolent Society (Netherbyres Appeal)

DRUM CASTLE, Drumoak, by Banchory &

(The National Trust for Scotland)

Walled garden of historic roses, opened June 1991. Roses representing 17th to 20th centuries at their best in mid-June to mid-July. Grounds contain arboretum, woodland walk, picnic area and farmland walk. Marquee teas. Plant and flower sale. Scottish Country Dancing. Garden craft stalls. Special activities for children.

Drum Castle is 10 miles west of Aberdeen and 8 miles east of Banchory on A93.

Garden & Grounds only £1.60   Children & OAPs £1.00

Castle, Garden and Grounds Adults £3.60   Concessions £2.40 Family ticket £9.60

SUNDAY 7th JULY 1.30 - 5 pm

40% to The Gardens Fund of The National Trust for Scotland

For other opening details see page 133

#GLASSEL LODGE, Banchory &

(Mr & Mrs M Welsh)

A developing garden containing flowers, kitchen garden and woodland.

Plant stall. 4 miles from A93 west of Banchory take right turn marked Glassel, Torphins, Lumphanan.

Admission £1.50 Children 50p

SUNDAY 14th JULY 2 - 5pm

40% to Friends of Cruickshank Botanic Garden

GLENBERVIE HOUSE, Drumlithie, Stonehaven
(Mrs C S Macphie)

Nucleus of present day house dates from the 15th century. Additions in 17th and 19th centuries. Walled garden with fine herbaceous and annual borders. Ornamental conservatory contains a dazzling display of interesting plants, also woodland garden. Teas. Plant and baking stalls. Drumlithie 1 mile. Garden 1½ miles off A90. NOT SUITABLE FOR WHEELCHAIRS.
Admission £1.75 Children 80p Cars free
SUNDAY 28th JULY 2 - 5 pm
40% to Kidney Research

HOUSE OF STRACHAN, Strachan, Banchory
(Dr & Mrs C McCance)

A mature garden of two acres, the grounds of what was Strachan Manse. It slopes south to the River Feugh and has a variety of roses, herbaceous borders and other plants and shrubs. Teas. Plant stall. On B976 on south side in centre of village of Strachan.
Admission £1.50
SUNDAY 21st JULY 2 - 5pm
40% to Friends of Crossroads

#INCHMARLO HOUSE GARDEN, Banchory   ♿ (limited)
(Skene Enterprises (Aberdeen) Ltd)

An ever changing 5 acre woodland garden, originally planted in the early Victorian era, featuring ancient Scots pines, Douglas firs, yews, beeches and a variety of other trees which form a dramatic background to an early summer riot of mature azaleas and rhododendrons producing a splendour of colour and scents.
Tea, coffee, homebakes - £2.00. From Aberdeen via North Deeside Road on A93 1m west of Banchory, turn right at main gate to Inchmarlo House.
Admission £2.00 Children free
SUNDAY 26th MAY 1.30 - 5pm
40% to Cancer Relief Macmillan Fund

SHOOTING GREENS, Strachan, Banchory ♿ (limited access)
(Mr & Mrs Donald Stuart-Hamilton)

Medium sized garden, landscaped with local stone, stems from terracing rough moorland near a burn and woodland glen. Short vistas and distant Grampian hills back raised, mixed, erica and alpine beds. Row of cairns and two small amphitheatres.
Beyond a small orchard, sloping to ponds, lie short walks by burn and through mixed and beech groves, one to a view point. Forestry Commission walks nearby. CARS PLEASE PARK ALONG PUBLIC ROAD. Route: On east side, near top of north-south Deeside link road between Potarch Hotel (2½ m) and Feughside Inn (1m) white stones at drive end; approximately 300 metres from car park for Forestry Commission's own Shooting Greens walks.
Admission £1.50 Children 50p
SUNDAY 28th APRIL 2 - 5 pm.   To 12th May by arrangement. Tel: 01330 850221.
40% to St Thomas's Church, Aboyne

LOCHABER, BADENOCH & STRATHSPEY

Joint District Organisers: **Mrs J Drysdale,** Ralia, Newtonmore PH20 1BD

Mrs J Ramsden, Dalchully, Laggan PH20 1BU

DATES OF OPENING

Ardtornish, Lochaline .... Daily 1 April – 31 October 10am – 6pm

Ardtornish, Lochaline .... Sunday 26 May   2 – 6pm
Achnacarry, Spean Bridge .... Sunday 26 May   2 - 5.30pm
Ard-Daraich, Ardgour .... Sunday 2 June   2 - 5pm
Ralia & Small Gardens in Newtonmore .... Sunday 30 June   2 - 5pm
Aberarder, Kinlochlaggan .... Sunday 22 September   2 – 5.30pm
Ardverikie, Kinlochlaggan .... Sunday 22 September   2 – 5.30pm

ABERARDER, Kinlochlaggan
(Lady Feilden)
Flower and kitchen garden. Marvellous views down Loch Laggan. Plant stall.
On A86 between Newtonmore and Spean Bridge at east end of Loch Laggan.
Combined admission with Ardverikie £1.50. Children under 12 free
SUNDAY 22nd SEPTEMBER 2 - 5.30 pm
40% to British Red Cross Society

ACHNACARRY, Spean Bridge   &
(Sir Donald & Lady Cameron of Lochiel)
An interesting wild garden in a lovely setting with a profusion of rhododendrons,
azaleas and flowers along the banks of the River Arkaig. A fine Georgian house full of
history. Clan Cameron Museum. Forest walks. Flower stall. Teas in Village Hall 200
yards from the house. Route: A82 Spean Bridge; left at Commando Memorial marked
Gairlochy. At Gairlochy turn right off B8005. Achnacarry is 7 miles from Spean Bridge.
Admission: House & garden £2.00 Children 50p.
SUNDAY 26th MAY 2 - 5.30pm
40% to Multiple Sclerosis Society (Lochaber)

ARD-DARAICH, Ardgour, by Fort William
(Major David & Lady Edith Maclaren)
Seven acre hill garden, in a spectacular setting, with many fine and uncommon
rhododendrons, an interesting selection of trees and shrubs and a large collection of
camellias, acers and sorbus. Home made teas in house. Cake and plant stall. Route:
west from Fort William, across the Corran Ferry and a mile on the right further west.
Admission £1.50 Children & OAPs 50p
SUNDAY 2nd JUNE 2 - 5pm
40% to Multiple Sclerosis Society (Fort William branch)

ARDTORNISH, Lochaline, Morvern
(Mrs John Raven)
Garden of interesting mature conifers, rhododendrons, deciduous trees and shrubs set set amidst magnificent scenery. Route A884. Lochaline 3 miles.
Admission £2.00 Children free OAPs £1.00
DAILY 1st APRIL to 31st OCTOBER 10 - 6pm
Donation to Scotland's Gardens Scheme
SUNDAY 26th MAY 2 - 6pm. Home made teas in main house 2 - 5pm
40% to Morvern Parish Church

ARDVERIKIE, Kinlochlaggan &
(Ardverikie Estate Company)
Lovely setting on Loch Laggan with magnificent trees. Walled garden with large collection of acers, shrubs and herbaceous. Architecturally interesting house. On A86 between Newtonmore and Spean Bridge - entrance at east end of Loch Laggan, by gate lodge over bridge. Home made cream teas.
Combined admission with Aberarder £1.50 Children under 12 free
SUNDAY 22nd SEPTEMBER 2 - 5.30 pm
40% to British Red Cross Society

RALIA LODGE (Mr & Mrs John Drysdale)
& Small Gardens in Newtonmore
Ralia is a relatively new garden with shrub borders, water garden and views of hills over loch. Various attractive village gardens also open. Home baked teas. Plant stall. A9 to southern Newtonmore turn, 300 yds., fork right, first entrance on left.
SUNDAY 30th JUNE 2 - 5pm
40% to British Red Cross Society

MIDLOTHIAN

District Organiser:	**The Hon Mrs C J Dalrymple,** OBE, Oxenfoord Mains, Dalkeith EH22 2PF
Area Organisers:	**Mrs George Burnet,** Rose Court, Inveresk
	Mrs H Faulkner, Currie Lee, Nr Pathhead EH37 5XB
	Mrs S MacMillan, Beechpark House, Broomieknowe, Lasswade EH18 1LN

DATES OF OPENING

Greenfield Lodge, Lasswade .... Sunday 10 March	2 – 5pm
Prestonhall, Pathhead .... Sunday 17 March	2 – 5pm
Greenfield Lodge, Lasswade .... Sunday 24 March	2 – 5pm
Arniston, Gorebridge .... Sunday 14 April	2 – 5.30pm
Prestonhall, Pathhead .... Sunday 21 April	2 – 6pm
Newhall, Carlops .... Sunday 28 April	2 - 5pm
Penicuik House, Penicuik .... Sunday 2 June	2-5.30pm
Newhall, Carlops .... Sunday 9 June	2 - 6pm
Borthwick Castle Hotel, Borthwick .... Sunday 28 July	2 - 6pm
Newhall, Carlops .... Sunday 18 August	2 - 6pm
SGS Plant Sale	
Oxenfoord Mains, Dalkeith .... Sunday 13 October	11am - 4pm

ARNISTON, Gorebridge ♿ (partly)
(Mrs Aedrian Dundas-Bekker)
William Adam Mansion House. Parklands. Sunken garden which was laid out in the late 18th century with bridges incorporating stones from old Parliament House. Tour of House £2.50 Teas. Route: B6372 Gorebridge 2 miles.
Admission 50p Children 25p
TUESDAYS, THURSDAYS & SUNDAYS from JULY to Mid-SEPTEMBER
Groups by appointment. Tel: 01875 830238
SUNDAY 14th APRIL 2 - 5.30pm
40% to The Thistle Foundation

#BORTHWICK CASTLE HOTEL, North Middleton
Garden of approx. 1 acre being created within mediaeval walls used as fortifications and dating from 1430. New garden features include herbaceous borders, rose and heather beds. Exhibitions of sculptures and of watercolours. History tours of the Castle. Cookery demonstrations. Outdoor teas. Route: Turn off A7 12m south of Edinburgh at North Middleton, 1m down lane.
Admission £1.50 Children 50p
SUNDAY 28th JULY 2 - 6pm
40% to Edinburgh Gynaecological Cancer Fund

GREENFIELD LODGE, Lasswade ♿
(Alan & Helen Dickinson)
A 1½ acre wooded garden with a very wide range of flowering shrubs, unusual herbaceous plants, ornamental grasses, alpines and bulbs, including the National Chionodoxa Collection. The garden is designed to give colour and interest throughout the year: hellebores, cyclamen, aquilegias, meconopsis, eryngiums, dieramas and gentians are well represented. Early 19th century bow-fronted house with later additions (not open). Teas. Plant stall. Parking. No dogs please. Off the Loanhead to Lasswade road (A768) at the end of Green Lane, off Church Road.
Admission £1.50 Careful children free.
First Tuesday of each month APRIL-SEPTEMBER incl. 2 - 5pm and throughout the year by appt., tel. 0131 663 9338 day before proposed visit.
SUNDAYS 10th & 24th MARCH 2 - 5pm
40% to Shelter (Scotland)

#NEWHALL, Carlops   ♿ (Walled garden only)
(The Orcome Trust)
Scene of Allan Ramsay's celebrated dramatic poem 'The Gentle Shepherd' and meeting place of the "Worthies", his patrons; glen of the North Esk with "Habbie's How", "Peggy's Pool" and "Craigie Bield". Parkland. Traditional 18th century Scottish walled garden; spring bulbs; mixed borders; shrubs; kitchen garden; lily pool; vine house with sturdy and aged wines. Teas. Some pot plants for sale at June & August openings. On A702 Edinburgh/Biggar, exactly half mile after Ninemileburn and 1 mile before Carlops. Gates on left.
Admission £1.50 Children 50p
SUNDAY 28th APRIL 2 - 5pm
SUNDAYS 9th JUNE & 18th AUGUST 2 - 6pm
40% to Children's Hospice Association Scotland

PENICUIK HOUSE, Penicuik   ♿
(Sir John D Clerk Bt)
Landscaped grounds with ornamental lakes, rhododendrons and azaleas. Plant stall. Home baked teas in house. On A766 road to Carlops. Penicuik 2miles.
Admission £1.00 Children 50p
SUNDAY 2nd JUNE 2 - 5.30pm
40% to Fairmile Marie Curie Centre

PRESTONHALL, Pathhead ♿
(Major & Mrs J H Callander)
Set in extensive parkland originally laid out in the 18th century. The mature park trees with their surrounding woodland and wild gardens are a wonderful setting for carpets of snowdrops in March and a profusion of daffodils and rhododendrons in April/May. Many new species of trees have been planted recently. Signed off A68 at Pathhead 25 minutes south east of Edinburgh.
Admission £1.50 Children 50p
SUNDAY 17th MARCH 2 - 5pm. Snowdrop Day
SUNDAY 21st APRIL 2 - 6pm. Daffodil Day. Teas.
20% to Malcolm Sargent Cancer Fund for Children
20% to Crichton Collegiate Church Trust

#THE MILL HOUSE, Temple
(Mrs C F Yannaghas)
A charming riverside garden with botanical interest throughout the year, including spring flowers, camomile lawn and interesting use of ground cover. A conservation area within Knights Templar enclave. Cream teas. Temple is 3 miles off A7 on B6372.
Admission £1.50
The second WEDNESDAY of each month APRIL - SEPTEMBER 2 - 5pm
40% to Temple Village Hall Fund

SGS PLANT SALE
A Bring and Buy Plant Sale will be held at Oxenfoord Mains, Dalkeith, on
SUNDAY 13th OCTOBER 11am - 4pm.
Route: 4 miles south of Dalkeith on A68, turn left for one mile on A6093.
Admission free.

MORAY & NAIRN

District Organiser: **Mrs H D P Brown,** Tilliedivie House, Relugas, Dunphail, Forres IV36 0QL

Hon. Treasurer: **Mr H D P Brown,** Tilliedivie House, Relugas, Dunphail, Forres IV36 0QL

DATES OF OPENING

Carestown Steading, Deskford	Sunday 2 June	2 - 5pm
Revack, Grantown-on-Spey	Wednesday 5 June	10am – 6pm
Dallas Lodge, Dallas	Sunday 9 June	2 – 6pm
Delnesmuir Residential Home, Nairn	Sunday 9 June	2 - 5pm
Gordonstoun, Duffus	Sunday 23 June	2 -5.30pm
Drummuir Castle Garden, by Keith	Sunday 21 July	2 – 5pm

#CARESTOWN STEADING, Deskford, Buckie
(Rora Paglieri)
An award winning steading conversion in a three acre rural garden reclaimed from wasteland in 1990 and still developing and maturing. The plants and flowers are native as far as possible and the few exotics have been present in Scotland for many years. The aim is for the gardens to look natural. The one example of manicured gardening is the 90 sq m. of courtyard with knot beds of box in the old Scottish tradition. Vegetable garden, orchard and ponds. Plant stall. Route: East off B9018 Cullen/Keith (Cullen 3m, Keith 9½ m). Follow SGS signs towards Milton and Carestown.
Admission £1.50 Children 50p
SUNDAY 2nd JUNE 2 - 5pm
All takings to Scotland's Gardens Scheme

DALLAS LODGE, Dallas, by Forres ⅙ (partly)
(David Houldsworth Esq)
Lawns and borders, azaleas, specimen trees and rhododendrons in natural woodland setting around lochs. Woodland walk. Tea in Houldsworth Institute, Dallas village. Entrance off B9010 6 miles from Forres.
Admission £1.50 Children 50p
SUNDAY 9th JUNE 2 - 6 pm
40% to Cancer Relief Macmillan Fund

DELNESMUIR RESIDENTIAL HOME, Nairn
(Mrs F J Macgillivray)
Woodland walk. Rhododendrons, azaleas. Well-kept lawns and shrubbery. Teas £1.50. Entrance off A96 Inverness road, 1 mile west of Nairn.
Admission £1.00 Children 50p
SUNDAY 9th JUNE 2 - 5 pm
40% to Childline

DRUMMUIR CASTLE GARDEN, by Keith
(Mr & Mrs Alex Gordon-Duff)
Traditional walled garden using organic methods to grow fruit, vegetables and herbs.
Plant stall. Five miles from Keith and Dufftown on B9014.
Admission £1.50 Children Under 12 Free
SUNDAY 21st JULY 2 - 5 pm
40% to Drummuir Community Association

GORDONSTOUN, Duffus, near Elgin &
(The Headmaster, Gordonstoun School)
School grounds; Gordonstoun House (Georgian House of 1775/6 incorporating earlier
17th century house built for 1st Marquis of Huntly) and School Chapel - both open.
Unique circle of former farm buildings known as the Round Square. Teas. Entrance off
B9012 4 miles from Elgin at Duffus village.
Admission £1.50 Children 50p
SUNDAY 23rd JUNE 2 - 5.30 pm
All takings to Scotland's Gardens Scheme

REVACK, Grantown-on-Spey & (partly)
(Lady Pauline Ogilvie-Grant)
Home of Lady Pauline Ogilvie-Grant, daughter of the late Countess of Seafield.
Beautifully laid out gardens and grounds with a wide variety of specimen trees and
shrubs amidst a tranquil setting. The walled vegetable garden offers spectacular views.
Orchid houses, for which Revack is famous, have been featured on the Beechgrove
Garden TV programme. Restaurant. Cafeteria. Plant sales. Gift shop. Children's play
area. Entrance off B970 Grantown-on-Spey/Nethybridge. Open all year, daily 10am-
6pm.
Last entry 5pm.
Admission £2.00 Children & OAPs £1.00 Family Ticket £5.00
WEDNESDAY 5th JUNE 10am - 6pm (Last entry 5pm)
40% to The Highland Hospice

PERTH & KINROSS

| *Joint District Organisers:* | **Mrs M E Hamilton,** Glencarse House, Glencarse PH2 7LF |
| | **Mrs Charles Moncrieff,** Easter Elcho, Rhynd PH2 8QQ |

Area Organisers:	**Mrs D J W Anstice,** Broomhill, Abernethy PH2 9LQ
	Mrs C Dunphie, Wester Cloquhat, Bridge of Cally PH10 7JP
	Mrs T J Hope Thomson, High Birches, Fairmount Road, Perth PH2 7AW
	Mrs Alastair Leslie, Seasyde House, Errol PH2 7TA
	Lady Livesay, Crosshill House, Strathallan, Auchterarder PH3 7LN
	Mrs Colin Maitland Dougall, Dowhill, Kelty, Fife KY4 0HZ
	Mrs Athel Price, Urlar Farm, Aberfeldy PH15 2EW

| *Hon. Treasurer:* | **Mrs J Bell,** Greenwood, Kinfauns, Perth PH2 7JZ |

DATES OF OPENING

Ardvorlich, Lochearnhead	11 May - 9 June	2 - 6pm
Bolfracks, Aberfeldy	Daily 1 April – 31 October	10am – 6pm
Cluny House, Aberfeldy	Daily 1 March – 31 October	10am – 6pm
Drummond Castle Gardens, Muthill ..	Daily May - October 2 - 6pm (last entrance 5pm)	
Lude, Blair Atholl................................	Wednesdays 26 June, 3, 10, 17, 24, 31 July,	
	& 7 August,	11am – 5pm
Scone Palace, Perth	5 April – 14 October:	9.30am – 5pm
Meikleour House, by Blairgowrie	Sunday 14 April	2 - 5pm
Glendoick, by Perth	Sunday 5 May	2 – 5pm
Branklyn, Perth	Sunday 12 May	9.30am – sunset
Glendoick, by Perth	Sunday 12 May	2 – 5pm
Meikleour House, by Blairgowrie	Sunday 12 May	2 - 5pm
Glendoick, by Perth	Sunday 19 May	2 – 5pm
Rossie, by Bridge of Earn	Sunday 19 May	2 - 6pm
Stobhall, by Perth	Sunday 19 May	2 - 6pm
Glendoick, by Perth	Sunday 26 May	2 – 5pm
Kinross Private Spring Gardens	Sat/Sun 1&2 June	2-5.30pm
Greenacres, Logiealmond	Sunday 2 June	2 – 5pm
Kennacoil House, Dunkeld	Sunday 2 June	2 – 6pm
Cloquhat Gardens, Bridge of Cally	Sunday 9 June	2 – 6pm
Meikleour House, by Blairgowrie	Sunday 9 June	2 - 5pm
Branklyn, Perth	Sunday 16 June	9.30am – sunset
Kirkton Craig, Abernyte	Sunday 23 June	2 - 5pm
Boreland, Killin	Sunday 21 July	2-5.30pm
Blairgowrie & Rattray Gardens	Sunday 4 August	1 – 6pm
Drummond Castle Gardens, Muthill	Sunday 4 August	2 – 6pm
Cluniemore, Pitlochry..	Sunday 11 August	2 – 5pm
Megginch Castle, Errol	Sunday 11 August	2 – 5pm
Bonskeid House, near Pitlochry	Sat/Sun 21&22 September	10.30-5pm
Meikleour House, by Blairgowrie	Sunday 20 October	2 - 5pm

ARDVORLICH, Lochearnhead
(Mr & Mrs Sandy Stewart)
Beautiful glen with rhododendrons (species and modern hybrids) grown in wild conditions amid oaks and birches. Gum boots advisable when wet.
On south Lochearn road 3m from Lochearnhead, 4½ m from St Fillans.
Admission £1.00 Children under 12 free
11th MAY to 9th JUNE incl. 2 - 6pm
40% to St Columba's Hospice

BLAIRGOWRIE & RATTRAY ₺ (partly)
The "Blair in Bloom" Committee would like to invite you to visit some colourful town gardens of varying sizes. Teas and Plant Stalls. Maps & tickets available from Tourist Information Centre, Wellmeadow, Blairgowrie. No dogs, except guide dogs, please.
Admission £2.00 Accompanied children under 12 free OAPs £1.00
SUNDAY 4th AUGUST 1 - 6pm
40% to Local Registered Charities

BOLFRACKS, Aberfeldy
(Mr J D Hutchison CBE)
Garden overlooking the Tay valley. Walled garden with borders of trees, shrubs and perennials. Burn garden with rhododendrons, azaleas, primulas, meconopsis, etc. in woodland setting. Masses of bulbs in spring. Good autumn colour. No dogs please. Limited range of plants for sale. Route: 2 miles west of Aberfeldy on A827. White gates and Lodge on left of road. Not suitable for wheelchairs.
Admission £2.00 Children under 16 free
DAILY 1st APRIL to 31st OCTOBER 10 am - 6 pm
Donation to Scotland's Gardens Scheme

#BONSKEID HOUSE, near Pitlochry
(YMCA Scottish National Council)
The house, formerly the property of George Freeland Barbour, has been run as a holiday and conference centre by the YMCA since 1921. The house and grounds (38 acres) were sited in 1800 by Alexander Stewart to take advantage of the dramatic views across the River Tummel, and for visitors to experience the romanticism of a baronial residence in a wild woodland setting. Woodland walks, some steep paths, wandering amongst mature exotic specimen trees and ponticum rhododendrons. After suffering many years of neglect, the grounds have now benefited from 12 months of an ongoing reclamation project. Flower beds under construction, walled garden reclaimed, rare breed animals, lovely autumn colours. Teas. Route: A9 Killiecrankie exit, 4 miles along B8019 Tummel Bridge road, on left hand side.
Admission £1.50 Children 50p
SATURDAY & SUNDAY 21st & 22nd SEPTEMBER 10.30am - 5pm
20% YMCA   20% to The Rare Breeds Survival Trust

BORELAND, Killin &
(Mrs Angus Stroyan)
A varied garden but with border the main feature. Very pretty walk along river leading to arboretum. Teas. Plant stall. Route: through Killin, first turning left over bridge after Bridge of Lochay Hotel. House approx. 2m on left.
Admission £1.50 Children over 12 50p
SUNDAY 21st JULY 2 - 5.30pm
40% to Cancer Research

BRANKLYN, Perth
(The National Trust for Scotland)
Rhododendrons, alpines, herbaceous and peat garden plants from all over the world. Cars free. Tea and coffee. On A85 Perth/Dundee road.
Admission £2.10 Children & OAPs £1.40
SUNDAY 12th MAY and SUNDAY 16th JUNE 9.30 am - sunset
40% to The Gardens Fund of The National Trust for Scotland
For other opening details see page 122

CLOQUHAT GARDENS, Bridge of Cally ♿ (partly)
Cloquhat. (Colonel Peter Dunphie CBE)
Fine views down to river. Azaleas, rhododendrons, shrubs. Woodland and burnside
gardens. Terrace with rock plants. Walled garden.
Wester Cloquhat. (Brigadier & Mrs Christopher Dunphie)
Small garden started in 1989. Splendid situation. Several mixed borders with wide
variety of shrubs and herbaceous plants. Heather bank. Teas and plant stall. No dogs
please. Turn off A93 just north of Bridge of Cally and follow yellow signs one mile.
Admission to both gardens £2.00 Children 50p
SUNDAY 9th JUNE 2 - 6 pm
40% to SSAFA

CLUNIEMORE, Pitlochry ♿
(Major Sir David & Lady Butter)
Water garden, rock garden. Woodlands in beautiful setting. Shrubs, herbaceous
borders, annual border and roses. Plant stall. Tea, biscuits and ice cream.
Parties by appointment any time. On A9 Pitlochry bypass.
Admission £2.00 Children under 16 free
SUNDAY 11th AUGUST 2 - 5pm
40% to The Pushkin Prizes in Scotland

CLUNY HOUSE, Aberfeldy
(Mr J & Mrs W Mattingley)
Woodland garden with many specimen trees, shrubs and rhododendrons, with
extensive views of Strathtay to Ben Lawers. An outstanding collection of primulas,
meconopsis, nomocharis, cardiocrinums and other Himalayan plants. Autumn colour.
Plant stall.
No dogs please. 3½ miles from Aberfeldy on Weem to Strathtay road.
Admission £2.00 Children under 16 free
DAILY 1st MARCH to 31st OCTOBER 10 am - 6 pm
Donation to Scotland's Gardens Scheme

DRUMMOND CASTLE GARDENS, Crieff ♿
(Grimsthorpe & Drummond Castle Trust Ltd)
The gardens of Drummond Castle were originally laid out in 1630 by John Drummond,
2nd Earl of Perth. In 1830 the parterre was changed to an Italian style. One of the most
interesting features is the multi-faceted sundial designed by John Mylne, Master Mason
to Charles I. The formal garden is said to be one of the finest in Europe and is the
largest of its type in Scotland. Open daily May to October 2 - 6 pm (last entrance 5 pm).
Entrance 2 miles south of Crieff on Muthill road (A822).
Admission £3.00   OAPs £2.00 Children £1.00
SUNDAY 4th AUGUST 2 - 6 pm. Teas, raffle, entertainments & stalls.
40% to British Limbless Ex-Servicemen's Association

GLENDOICK, Perth 🕭 (partly)
(Mr & Mrs Peter Cox & family)

Classic Georgian house about 1746 (not open). Garden full of interesting plants and trees, with extended area of meandering paths to explore in the famous rhododendron woodland. Nursery also open. No dogs please. Refreshments at Tea/Coffee shop at Garden Centre, open 9.30am-5 pm. On (A85) A90 Perth/Dundee road. Glencarse 2 miles, Perth 8 miles, Dundee 11 miles.
Admission £2.00 Children under 5 free
SUNDAYS 5th, 12th, 19th, 26th MAY 2 - 5 pm
40% to World Wide Fund for Nature

GREENACRES, Logiealmond
(Mr & Mrs M J L Taylor)

Cottage garden of half an acre; 500 ft above sea level but sheltered. Filled with collectors' plants and shrubs, pond with waterplants, ferns a speciality. Spectacular views of surrounding countryside. Bird habitat a priority. Plant stall. 10m north west of Perth. From A9 take first exit, B8063, past Battleby, 6m to Chapelhill, 600 yards past pub. Greenacres is on south (left hand side) of road.
Admission £1.50 Children under 16 50p
SUNDAY 2nd JUNE 2 - 5pm
40% to St Ninian's Cathedral Development Campaign

KENNACOIL HOUSE, Dunkeld
(Mrs Walter Steuart Fothringham)

Informal to wild garden with herbaceous border, shrubs, rhododendrons and azaleas on hillside with exceptional view. Burn with water garden. Teas. Plant stall. No dogs please. Dunkeld 3 miles, off Crieff road A822.
Admission £1.50 Children under 12 50p
SUNDAY 2nd JUNE 2 - 6 pm
40% to Perth & Perthshire Fund for the Elderly

#KINROSS PRIVATE SPRING GARDENS
Achaneoir, Station Road (Tom & Elizabeth Fraser)
Large walled garden specialising in bamboos, pines, rhododendrons and meconopsis.
Hayfield Wildlife Garden, Station Road
1½ acres. Variety of habitats, including spring flowering meadow.
Mansfield, 17 Bowton Road (Martin & Irene Ellam)
Many interesting features including shrubberies, raised beds, pond and pergola.

Home baked teas. Plant stall. Station Road joins centre of Kinross with M90. Both gardens near tennis courts by primary school. Bowton Road near town centre via Swansacre and School Wynd.
Admission £1.50 Children & OAPs 50p
SATURDAY & SUNDAY 1st & 2nd JUNE 2 - 5.30pm
20% to Scottish Wildlife Trust (Fife branch)
20% to Hayfield Wildlife Garden Charitable Assn.

#KIRKTON CRAIG, Abernyte
(Mr & Mrs Rodney Berger)
Old walled garden of 0.75 acre, 400ft above the Tay. Mixed borders with use made of the walls for climbing plants amongst old fruit trees. Good plant stall. Take B953 off A90 signed Abernyte. Turn right in village (sign to church). Park on road.
Admission £1.50 Children 50p
SUNDAY 23rd JUNE 2 - 5pm
40% to Scottish Spina Bifida Association

LUDE, Blair Atholl &
(Mr & Mrs W G Gordon)
A "secret" walled garden built c1815 which encloses herbaceous borders, an arboretum, a peony border, shrubs and many varieties of old roses. Stunning views to the hills. Blair Atholl 1¼ miles, entrance is opposite Tilt Hotel.
Admission £1.50 Children free
WEDNESDAYS 26th JUNE, 3rd, 10th, 17th, 24th, 31st JULY, 7th AUGUST 11am-5pm
40% to the two Churches in Blair Atholl

MEGGINCH CASTLE, Errol &
(Captain Drummond of Megginch & Baroness Strange)
15th century turreted castle (not open) with Gothic courtyard and pagoda dovecote. 1,000 year old yews and topiary work in natural surroundings. Colourful annual border in walled garden. Astrological garden. Memorabilia from "Rob Roy" filmed in the courtyard. Water garden (projected) On A85 between Perth (9½m) and Dundee (12m). Look for Lodge on south side of road.
Admission £2.00 Children free
SUNDAY 11th AUGUST 2 - 5 pm
40% to All Saints Church, Glencarse

MEIKLEOUR HOUSE, by Blairgowrie & **(with assistance)**
(The Marquis of Lansdowne)
Water and woodland garden on the banks of the River Tay. Fine trees, specie rhododendrons and lovely autumn colours. No dogs please. Entrance to water and woodland garden 300 yards from car parks. Enter via Meikleour Lodge, 5 miles south of Blairgowrie off A93 at its junction with the Stanley/Kinclaven Bridge road.
Admission £1.50 Children free
SUNDAYS 14th APRIL, 12th MAY, 9th JUNE, 20th OCTOBER 2 - 5pm
40% to R N I B (Scotland)

ROSSIE, Forgandenny, by Bridge of Earn &
(Mr & Mrs David B Nichol)
Fine trees, flowering shrubs, rhododendrons and woodland walks among the bluebells. Teas in house. Plant stall. Strathallan pipe band. Forgandenny ¼m on B935 between Bridge of Earn and Dunning. Buses from Perth and south, via Bridge of Earn & Dunning, stop in village and, by request, at Rossie gates.
Admission £1.50 Children under 12 free
SUNDAY 19th MAY 2 - 6pm
40% to Forgandenny Playing Fields Assn.

SCONE PALACE, Perth ♿
(The Earl of Mansfield)
Extensive and well laid out grounds and a magnificent pinetum dating from 1848; there is
a Douglas Fir raised from the original seed sent from America in 1824. The Woodland
Garden has attractive walks amongst the rhododendrons and azaleas and leads into the
Monks' Playgreen and Friar's Den of the former Abbey of Scone. The Palace of Scone
lies adjacent to the Moot Hill where the Kings of Scots were crowned. Full catering by
the Palace staff. Adventure playground. Special rates for season tickets and parties.
Route A93. Perth 2 miles.
Admission: Palace & Grounds £4.70 Children £2.60 OAPs £3.90 Family £13.50
FRIDAY 5th APRIL to MONDAY 14th OCTOBER 9.30am - 5pmdaily
Donation to Scotland's Gardens Scheme

STOBHALL, by Perth ♿
(The Earl & Countess of Perth)
Group of early and mediaeval buildings, including castle and chapel with painted
ceiling, on ridge high above River Tay. Site of dwelling houses since 14th century,
associated with two Queens of Scotland. Early topiary garden, also wild garden and
walk in woodland glen. Terrace walk below castle. Refreshments. 1½ m north of
Guildtown on A93 midway between Perth and Blairgowrie.
Admission to gardens and chapel £2.00 Children £1.00
SUNDAY 19th MAY 2 - 6pm
40% to the Innerpeffray Library

RENFREW & INVERCLYDE

Joint District Organisers:	**Mrs J R Hutton,** Auchenclava, Finlaystone, Langbank PA14 6TJ
	Mrs Daphne Ogg, Nittingshill, Kilmacolm PA13 4SG
Area Organisers:	**Lady Denholm,** Newton of Bell Trees, Lochwinnoch PA12 4JL
	Mr J Wardrop, St Kevins, Victoria Road, Paisley PA2 9PT
Hon. Treasurer:	**Mrs Jean Gillan,** 28 Walkerston Avenue, Largs KA30 8ER

DATES OF OPENING

Mosswood, Kilmacolm .... May & June by appointment

Ardgowan, Inverkip	Sunday 11 February	2 – 5pm
Finlaystone, Langbank	Sunday 14 April	2 – 5pm
Renfrew Central Nursery	Sat & Sun 25/26 May	1 – 5pm
Crossways, Bishopton	Sunday 26 May	1 - 5pm
Carruth Plant Sale, Bridge of Weir	Sunday 2 June	2 - 5pm
Parklea Nursery, Port Glasgow	Sunday 9 June	11am – 4pm
Lunderston, Ardgowan	Sunday 23 June	2 – 5pm
Uplawmoor Gardens	Sunday 7 July	2 - 6pm
Bridge of Weir Gardens	Sunday 14 July	2 - 5pm
Elderslie Gardens	Sunday 21 July	2 - 5pm

ARDGOWAN, Inverkip ♿ (not advisable if wet)
(Sir Houston and Lady Shaw-Stewart)
Woodland walks carpeted with snowdrops. (Strong footwear advised). Tea in house.
Snowdrop stall, souvenirs, home produce and plant stall. Inverkip 1½ miles.
Glasgow/Largs buses in Inverkip.
Admission £1.00 Children under 10 free
SUNDAY 11th FEBRUARY 2 - 5 pm
40% to Inverkip Guides Group

#BRIDGE OF WEIR GARDENS
Three gardens very close to each other providing a wide variety of interest.
Torbreck, Eldin Place (Mr & Mrs Mitchell)
Cottage style garden with shrubs, conifers, herbaceous and annual plants, designed to
give colour throughout the year. Also a variety of wall trained fruit trees.
40% to Cancer Research
Rossarden, Eldin Place (Mrs Campbell)
Small colourful garden with rockery and herbaceous borders.
40% to Cancer Research
6 The Grove, (Mr & Mrs J R Gilchrist)
Small garden packed with plants, mainly herbaceous and shrubs specialising in
variegated and coloured foliage including grasses and bonsai.
40% to Save the Children Fund
Plant stalls. Teas. Take the Kilbarchan road out of Bridge of Weir, right into Ranfurly
Road and left into Eldin Place. The Grove is just round the corner.
Admission £2.00 includes all gardens.
SUNDAY 14th JULY 2 - 5pm

CARRUTH, Bridge of Weir ♿
(Mr & Mrs Charles MacLean)
PLANT SALE. Big selection of herbaceous, herbs and shrubs etc., in lovely country
setting. Beautiful trees and many different rhododendrons. Teas. Woodland walking.
Access from B786 Kilmacolm/Lochwinnoch road.
Admission £1.00
SUNDAY 2nd JUNE 2 - 5pm
40% to Cancer Relief Macmillan Fund

#CROSSWAYS, by Bishopton ♿
(James Mackie & Gerald Lloyd-Gray)
A new garden of 11 years, level and just over one acre. Mainly rhododendrons and
azaleas. 80ft lily pond, bamboos, gunnera and 'walk-in' cloche. Tea and biscuits.
Plant stall. Roadside car parking. From Bishopton proceed up hill following Formakin
signs. Crossways is first on left and the first of 3 houses known as 'The Three Bears',
prior to Bishopton cemetery.
Admission £1.00 OAPs 50p Accompanied children free
SUNDAY 26th MAY 1 - 5pm
40% to Erskine Hospital

ELDERSLIE GARDENS
Three contrasting gardens within easy walking distance.
49 Main Road (Mr & Mrs Robert Mitchell)
Low maintenance, attractively landscaped, south facing garden. Rockeries, fish pond, formal bedding, ornamental paving. Plant stall. No dogs please.
Knaresby, 6 Newton Avenue ⑁ (Mr & Mrs Iain McAlpine)
Spacious walled garden with wide range of interest; variety of trees and shrubs, large herbaceous border, rock wall, annual bedding plants etc. Plant & baking stalls.
No dogs please.
Boulouris, 23 Newton Avenue (Mr & Mrs William L Campbell)
A simple area gently sloping towards the golf course. Variety of rhododendrons, azalea moliis, potentillas and other acid loving plants. Bedding annuals predominate in summer giving a colourful display. Plant stall.

Gardens are at east end of Elderslie. Entering Elderslie from Paisley, Newton Avenue is first on left. Golf course bus stop just west of 49 Main Road. Cars should be parked in Newton Avenue or Newton Drive for all three gardens.
Teas available at Brubecks, 133 Main Road, Elderslie.
Admission £2.00 includes all gardens.
SUNDAY 21st JULY 2 - 5pm
40% to Children First

FINLAYSTONE, Langbank ⑁
(Mr & Mrs George G MacMillan)
Historic connection with John Knox and Robert Burns. Richly varied gardens with unusual plants overlooking the Clyde. Profusion of daffodils and early rhododendrons.
Waterfalls & pond. Woodland walks with play and picnic areas, fort and 'Eye-opener' Centre. Ranger service. Plant stall. Teas in Celtic Tree.
Admission to House: £1.50 Children & OAPs £1.00. Langbank station 1 mile.
On A8 west of Langbank, 10 minutes by car west of Glasgow Airport.
Admission £2.00 Children & OAPs £1.20
SUNDAY 14th APRIL 2 - 5 pm
20% to Quarrier's Village   20% to Erskine Hospital

LUNDERSTON, Ardgowan, Inverkip ⑁
(Dr J L Kinloch)
Landscaped garden with fine views across the Firth of Clyde. Wide selection of plants including rhododendron bank, heather garden, roses, herbaceous and well laid out vegetable garden. Plant stall. Teas. Enter Ardgowan at North Lodge and follow signs.
Admission £1.50 Children over 10 & OAPs £1.00
SUNDAY 23rd JUNE 2 - 5 pm
20% to Ardgowan Hospice   20% to Erskine Hospital

MOSSWOOD, Glenmosston Road, Kilmacolm
(Mrs A Fairbairn)
A pretty and secluded garden full of spring and early summer colour. Primulas, rhododendrons, a rockery made in natural rock, established trees and a lily pond.
Personally conducted tour. M8, Johnstone, Bridge of Weir, Kilmacolm.
Admission £2.00
MAY and JUNE by appointment: 01505 872493
40% to SANE

PARKLEA NURSERY, Port Glasgow ♿
(Inverclyde District Council)
Local authority glasshouses and nursery complex producing bedding plants, flowering and foliage pot plants. Teas, plant stall and other attractions. A8 Greenock road, first round-about at east side of Port Glasgow, 3rd exit, signposted Parklea Playing Fields.
Admission £1.00 Children 50p
SUNDAY 9th JUNE 11am - 4pm
40% to Local Registered Charities

RENFREW CENTRAL NURSERY, Hawkhead Road, Paisley ♿
(Renfrew District Council)
Three-quarters of an acre under glass, intensively cropped, associated with Open Day demonstrations. Exhibitions of related crafts, countryside interpretation etc. Entertainments etc. Tea served in marquee. Plant stall.
Admission £1.00 Children & OAPs 50p
SATURDAY & SUNDAY 25th & 26th MAY 1 - 5 pm
40% to Erskine Hospital

#UPLAWMOOR GARDENS
A group of 6 varied gardens 450-500ft above sea level, off the A736 Glasgow/Irvine, 5m southwest of Barrhead and 2m north of Lugton. Entering from Lugton end of village the gardens are:
Crioch ♿ partly (Prof.& Mrs J A M Inglis) Pedestrian access from Neilston Rd. Approx. 3 acre garden created 1969 with open outlook, woodland walk, lawns, shrubs, Scandinavian summer house. Access to Pollick Glen. Plant stall.
11 Neilston Road (Miss A D Baker) A sloping garden consisting of shrubs, perennials, annuals and vegetables.
Westleigh, Neilston Road (Mr & Mrs Gibson) Good sized garden with trees, shrubs & lily pond.
37 Neilston Road ♿ (Mr & Mrs D Ritson) Relatively young garden with wide variety of shrubs, herbaceous plants and water feature.
5 Tannoch Road (Mr & Mrs Heywood) Opp. village church. Small well kept garden.
Woodlands, Birchwood Road. ♿ partly (Mr & Mrs J West) Moderately sized garden being redeveloped. Long mixed border, old fashioned roses, fuchsias and small rhododendron/woodland area. Plant stall.
Teas (£1.00) at Caldwell Parish Church, Neilston Road. Open to visitors daily.
Admission £2.00 to include all gardens Children under 14 free
SUNDAY 7th JULY 2 - 6pm
40% to Caldwell Parish Church and Accord Hospice

ROSS, CROMARTY, SKYE & INVERNESS

District Organiser: **Lady Lister-Kaye,** Aigas House, Beauly IV4 7AD

Area Organisers: **Mrs Robin Fremantle,** Fannyfield, Evanton IV16 9XA

Hon. Treasurer: **Mr Kenneth Haselock,** 2 Tomich, Strathglass, by Beauly IV4 7LZ

DATES OF OPENING

Abriachan Garden Nursery	February – November	9am – dusk
Aigas House & Field Centre	Mid June – September	
Attadale, Strathcarron	1 April – 1 Oct (not Suns)	10am–1pm
Brin School Fields, Flichity	Daily June – September	8.30am – 7pm
	Sundays 2 – 5pm	
Coiltie, Divach, Drumnadrochit	Daily June - August	12 - 7pm
Dunvegan Castle, Isle of Skye	25 March - 31 October	10am-5.30pm
Glamaig, Braes, Isle of Skye	Daily Easter – mid-September	
Leckmelm Shrubbery & Arboretum	Daily 1 April – 30 Sept	10am– 6pm
Sea View, Dundonnell	Daily May – September	
Tournaig, Poolewe	By appointment	

Inverewe, Poolewe	Saturday 27 April	9.30am – sunset
Allangrange, Munlochy	Sunday 12 May	2 – 5.30pm
House of Gruinard, by Laide	Saturday 25 May	2 – 6pm
Laggan House, Scaniport	Sunday 26 May	2 – 5pm
Tournaig, Poolewe	Wednesday 29 May	2 – 6pm
Attadale, Strathcarron	Saturday 1 June	2 – 6pm
Dundonnell, by Little Loch Broom	Thursday 6 June	2 – 5.30pm
Lochalsh Woodland Garden, Balmacara	Saturday 8 June	1 – 5.30pm
Brahan, Dingwall	Sunday 9 June	2 – 5.30pm
Dundonnell, by Little Loch Broom	Wednesday 12 June	2 – 5.30pm
Allangrange, Munlochy	Sunday 16 June	2 – 5.30pm
Kyllachy, Tomatin	Sunday 16 June	2 – 5.30pm
Dundonnell, by Little Loch Broom	Thursday 4 July	2 – 5.30pm
Dundonnell, by Little Loch Broom	Wednesday 10 July	2 – 5.30pm
Aberchalder Lodge, Invergarry	Sunday 14 July	2 - 6pm
Allangrange, Munlochy	Sunday 14 July	2 – 5.30pm
House of Gruinard, by Laide	Wednesday 17 July	2 – 6pm
Inverewe, Poolewe	Sunday 28 July	9.30am – sunset
Tournaig, Poolewe	Wednesday 7 August	2 – 6pm
Glencalvie, by Ardgay	Sunday 25 August	2 - 6pm

ABRIACHAN GARDEN NURSERY, Loch Ness Side
(Mr & Mrs Davidson)
An outstanding garden. Over 2 acres of exciting plantings, with winding paths through native woodlands. Seasonal highlights - hellebores, primulas, meconopsis, hardy geraniums and colour themed summer beds. Views over Loch Ness.
Admission by collecting box. Adults £1.00
FEBRUARY to NOVEMBER 9 am - dusk

ABERCHALDER LODGE, Invergarry
(Miss Jean Ellice)
Dell walk with specimen rhododendrons, planted in early 1900s. Azaleas. Herbaceous garden with superb views of Loch Oich. Ornamental pheasants, kitchen garden, pea fowl, wishing well. Teas (£1.20). Bring & buy Produce and Plant stall.
Route: A82 Fort William/Inverness midway between Invergarry and Fort Augustus.
Admission £1.50 Children & OAPs 50p
SUNDAY 14th JULY 2 - 6pm
40% to Scottish Society for the Prevention of Cruelty to Animals

AIGAS HOUSE AND FIELD CENTRE, by Beauly
(Sir John and Lady Lister-Kaye)
Aigas has a woodland walk overlooking the Beauly River with a collection of named Victorian specimen trees now being restored and extended with a garden of rockeries, herbaceous borders and shrubberies. The house is open to the public for the Field Centre shop and teas and coffees - home baking a speciality. There is also a 1½ mile nature trail and rainbow trout fishing on Aigas Loch. Route: 4½ miles from Beauly on A831 Cannich/Glen Affric road.
Admission from £1.50
Mid JUNE to SEPTEMBER
Donation to Scotland's Gardens Scheme

ALLANGRANGE, Munlochy, Black Isle &
(Major Allan Cameron)
A formal and a wild garden containing flowering shrubs, trees and plants, especially rhododendrons, shrub roses, meconopsis and primulas. Plants for sale. Exhibition of botanical paintings by Elizabeth Cameron. Teas in house. Inverness 5 miles.
Signposted off A9.
Admission £1.50
SUNDAYS 12th MAY, 16th JUNE and 14th JULY 2 - 5.30 pm
40% to Highland Hospice

ATTADALE, Strathcarron
(Mr & Mrs Ewen Macpherson)
Five acres of old rhododendrons, azaleas and unusual shrubs in woodland setting with views of Skye and the sea. Water gardens, woodland walk and sunken formal garden.
On A890 opposite village of Lochcarron.
Admission £1.50 Children & OAPs 75p
1st APRIL - 1st OCTOBER 10am - 1pm, closed Sundays
SATURDAY 1st JUNE 2 - 6 pm   Teas, plant stall
40% to British Red Cross Society

BRAHAN, Dingwall
(Mr & Mrs A Matheson)
Wild garden, dell with azaleas and rhododendrons. Arboretum with labelled trees and river walk. Home made teas in house. Maryburgh 1½ miles. Take road west from Maryburgh roundabout.
Admission £1.50 Children free
SUNDAY 9th JUNE 2 - 5.30 pm
40% to Highland Hospice

BRIN SCHOOL FIELDS, Flichity, by Farr &
(Mr & Mrs A Mackenzie)
Specialist herb garden and nursery situated 700ft. above sea level beneath the dramatic backdrop of Brin Rock. Garden divided into many smaller gardens, including edible flowers garden, children's herb garden, knot garden, cottage garden, wildflower gardens, 'Good Companions' garden, Mediterranean conservatory etc. Over 300 varieties of herb and wild flower plants available. The Victorian Schoolroom Shop sells herb-related books, gifts, seeds, crafts, teas and light lunches. (Lunch bookings recommended, tel: 01808 521288). Inverness 15 miles, Farr 4½ miles. 7 miles from A9 junction at Daviot. On B851 Daviot/Fort Augustus road.
Leaflet & 'Walkman' tape guide available for donation
OPEN DAILY JUNE - SEPTEMBER 8.30am - 7pm. Sundays 2 - 5pm.
Donation to Scotland's Gardens Scheme

#COILTIE, Divach, Drumnadrochit
(Gillian & David Nelson)
A wooded garden, an amalgamation of a Victorian flower garden abandoned 60 years ago and a walled field with a large moraine, which has been made over the past 15 years. Development work still in progress. Many trees, old and new mixed shrubs and herbaceous borders, roses, wall beds. No dogs please. Off A82 at Drumnadrochit. Take road signposted Divach uphill 2 miles. Beyond Divach Lodge, 150m.
Admission £1.50 Small children free
OPEN DAILY JUNE - AUGUST 12 - 7pm
20% to Scotland's Gardens Scheme   20% to Amnesty International

---

DUNDONNELL, by Little Loch Broom
(Mr Alan and Mr Neil Roger)
Garden includes a collection of bonsai, prehistoric yew tree and ancient holly about 1600 AD. Tea. Plants for sale. No dogs in garden, on leads in arboretum. Dundonnell is on Little Loch Broom 31 miles west of Garve. Ullapool 24 miles.
Admission £1.50 Children 50p
THURSDAY 6th JUNE, WEDNESDAY 12th JUNE,
THURSDAY 4th JULY, WEDNESDAY 10th JULY 2 - 5.30 pm
40% to the Army Benevolent Fund and the Police Dependants Fund

DUNVEGAN CASTLE, Isle of Skye
Dating from the 13th century and continuously inhabited by the Chiefs of MacLeod, this romantic fortress stronghold occupies a magnificent lochside setting. The gardens, originally laid out in the 18th century, have been extensively replanted and include lochside walks, woodlands and water gardens. Licensed restaurant. Two craft shops. clan exhibition. Seal colony. Loch boat trips. Admission to Castle and Garden inclusive £4.50, students, OAPs & parties £4.00, children £2.50. Dunvegan village 1mile, 23 miles west of Portree.
Admission to gardens: £3.00 Children £1.50
Monday 25th MARCH - Thursday 31st OCTOBER 10am - 5.30pm. Last entry 5pm
Donation to Scotland's Gardens Scheme

GLAMAIG, Braes, Portree, Isle of Skye
(Mr & Mrs R Townsend)
Two acres of mixed wild and informal garden with burn, waterfalls and extensive views of sea, islands and mountains. Large collection of unusual shrubs, rhododendrons, olearias etc. Primulas,herbaceous and rock garden. Some plants for sale. 7 miles from Portree at end of B883.
Admission £1.00 OAPs 50p
OPEN DAILY EASTER TO MID-SEPTEMBER
Donation to Scotland's Gardens Scheme

#GLENCALVIE, by Ardgay &
(Glencalvie Estate)
Approx. 5 acres of lakeside, woodland and walled gardens. Newly planted (5 years) with continuing programme. Mainly shrubs, herbaceous and marsh plants. Riverside walk. Teas. Plant stall. From Ardgay follow signs to Croick, turn left at phone box and then second drive on left.
Admission £1.50 Children and OAPs £1.00
SUNDAY 25th AUGUST 2 - 6pm
40% to Carron Charitable Trust

HOUSE OF GRUINARD, by Laide
(The Hon Mrs Angus Maclay)
Wonderful west coast views. Herbaceous and shrub borders and water garden. Large variety of plants for sale.
Admission £1.50 Children under 16 free
SATURDAY 25th MAY & WEDNESDAY 17th JULY 2 - 6pm
40% to Highland Hospice

INVEREWE, Poolewe &
(The National Trust for Scotland)
Garden started in 1862 by Osgood Mackenzie. Eucalyptus, rhododendrons, azaleas and many Chilean and South African plants. Himalayan lilies and many other rare plants. Visitor centre, shop and self-service restaurant.
Admission £3.60 Children & OAPs £2.40 Family Ticket £9.60
SATURDAY 27th APRIL and SUNDAY 28th JULY 9.30 - sunset
40% to The Gardens Fund of the National Trust for Scotland
For further opening details see page 128

KYLLACHY, Tomatin &
(The Rt Hon Lord & Lady Macpherson)
Rhododendrons (mainly white), azaleas, meconopsis, primulas, delphiniums, heather beds, herbaceous, alpines, iris. Water garden with stream and ponds. Walled vegetable garden. Plant stall. Tea. No dogs please. Cars free. A9 to Tomatin, turn off to Findhorn Bridge, turn west to Coignafearn. Kyllachy House one mile on right.
Admission £1.50 Children & OAPs 50p. Free car parking.
SUNDAY 16th JUNE 2 - 5.30 pm
40% to The Highland Hospice

LAGGAN HOUSE, Scaniport
(Mr & Mrs Anthony Haig)
Rhododendrons, azaleas, flowering shrubs and woodland walks. Tea. Plant stall. Inverness 4 miles, on B862 Dores road.
Admission £1.50 Children free
SUNDAY 26th MAY 2 - 5 pm
40% to St Andrew's Cathedral, Inverness

LECKMELM SHRUBBERY & ARBORETUM, by Ullapool
(Mr & Mrs Peter Troughton)
The arboretum, planted in the 1870s, is full of splendid trees, specie rhododendrons, azaleas and shrubs. Warmed by the Gulf Stream, this tranquil woodland setting has an alpine garden and paths which lead down to the sea.
Parking in walled garden. Situated by the shore of Loch Broom 3 miles south of Ullapool on the A835 Inverness/Ullapool road.
Admission £1.00 Children under 16 free
OPEN DAILY 1st APRIL to 30th SEPTEMBER 10 am - 6 pm
20% to The Highland Hospice 20% to Scotland's Gardens Scheme

LOCHALSH WOODLAND GARDEN, Balmacara
(The National Trust for Scotland)
Passed to the Trust in 1953; main rhododendron planting by Euan Cox in the 1950's. A garden in the making, with developing collections of Rhododendron, bamboo, ferns, Fuchsia and Hydrangea; mature beeches, oaks, pines and larches. Teas at Lochalsh House. On the shores of Loch Alsh, signposted off A87, 3m east of Kyle of Lochalsh.
Admission £1.00 Children 50p
SATURDAY 8th JUNE 1 - 5.30 pm
40% to The Gardens Fund of The National Trust for Scotland
For other opening details see page 133

SEA VIEW GARDEN GALLERY, Durnamuck, Dundonnell &
(Simone & Ian Nelson)
Small, ½ acre cottage garden spectacularly positioned on the side of Little Loch Broom. The flourishing result of one woman's ongoing contest with virgin moor and the elements. Regret no dogs. Limited parking. gallery - Ian Nelson watercolours and Jack Reeves woodturning. Plant stall. Refreshments available at the Dundonnell Hotel, 6 miles away. Signed off the main A832 Gairloch /Dundonnell road at Badcaul for one mile.
Admission £1.00 Children free with adults
Daily MAY to SEPTEMBER
20% to Dundonnell Area Community Events 20% to Cancer Relief Macmillan Fund

TOURNAIG, Poolewe ♿ (partly)
(Lady Horlick)
Woodland, herbaceous and water garden. Plant stall. Tea in house. 1½ miles north of
Inverewe Garden, Poolewe, on main road. Can be viewed at any time on request.
Tel: 01445 781250 or 339.
Admission £1.50 Children under 12 free
WEDNESDAYS 29th MAY and 7th AUGUST 2 - 6 pm
20% to St John's Ambulance   20% to Highland Handicapped Child Centre

ROXBURGH

District Organiser:	**Mrs M D Blacklock,** Stable House, Maxton, St Boswells TD6 0EX
Area Organisers:	**The Hon Moyra Campbell,** Scraesburgh, Jedburgh TD8 6QR
Hon. Treasurer:	**Mr J Mackie,** Bank of Scotland, Newton St Boswells TD6 0PG

DATES OF OPENING

Floors Castle, Kelso .... Daily Easter to end September   10.30am – 5.30pm
October: Sundays & Wednesdays   10.30am – 4.30pm

Mertoun, St Boswells .... Sunday 2 June   2 – 6pm
Benrig, Benrig Cottage, Mansfield House
& Stable House, St Boswells .... Sunday 30 June   2 – 6pm
Corbet Tower, Morebattle .... Sunday 14 July   2 – 6pm
Monteviot, Jedburgh .... Sunday 21 July   2 – 5pm
Yetholm Village Gardens .... Sunday 4 August   2 – 6pm

BENRIG COTTAGE, St Boswells ♿
(Mrs J E Triscott)
A small garden incorporating roses, herbaceous plants and a small vegetable area. New
rose arbour. JOINT OPENING WITH BENRIG, MANSFIELD HOUSE and STABLE
HOUSE SITUATED ON THE SAME ROAD. Plant stall and cream teas available at
Stable House. Parking at Benrig and Mansfield House for all four gardens. St Boswells:
two minutes from A68 on the A699 to Kelso.
Admission £2.00, includes all gardens..
SUNDAY 30th JUNE 2 - 6 pm
20% to Capability Borders   20% to St Boswells Parish Church

BENRIG, St Boswells ♿
(Mr & Mrs Nigel Houldsworth)
Semi-walled garden with shrub roses and herbaceous plants. Magnificent views of the River Tweed. Play area for toddlers. Cake stall.
JOINT OPENING WITH BENRIG COTTAGE, STABLE HOUSE and MANSFIELD HOUSE, SITUATED ON THE SAME ROAD. Plant stall and cream teas available at Stable House. Parking at Benrig and Mansfield House for all four gardens. St Boswells: 2 minutes from A68 on the A699 to Kelso.
Admission £2.00, includes all gardens.
SUNDAY 30th JUNE 2 - 6 pm
20% to Capability Borders   20% to St Boswells Parish Church

CORBET TOWER, Morebattle
(Mr & Mrs G H Waddell)
Scottish baronial house (1896) set in parkland in the foothills of the Cheviots. Garden includes formal parterre with old fashioned roses. Traditional walled garden with herbaceous borders, herbs and vegetables. Woodland and water garden. Teas. Plant and vegetable stall. From A68 Jedburgh road take A698, at Eckford B6401 to Morebattle, then road marked Hownam.
Admission £1.50 Children under 14 free
SUNDAY 14th JULY 2 - 6 pm
40% to Jennifer Fund (Child Leukaemia Fund)

FLOORS CASTLE, Kelso ♿
(The Duke of Roxburghe)
Floors Castle is situated in beautiful Borders country, overlooking Kelso and the River Tweed. Extensive gardens, grounds and children's play area. Ample parking facilities. Garden Centre & Coffee Shop open daily 10.30 am - 5.30 pm; also Castle, grounds & restaurant. (Last admission to House 4.45 pm). Nearest town Kelso.
Open Daily EASTER to end SEPTEMBER 10.30am - 5.30pm
OCTOBER: Sundays & Wednesdays 10.30am - 4.30 pm
Donation to Scotland's Gardens Scheme

MANSFIELD HOUSE, St Boswells
(Mr & Mrs D M Forsyth)
18th century manse sitting in one acre of established garden, containing mixed planting of trees, shrubs and clematis. Interesting traditional vegetable garden. JOINT OPENING WITH BENRIG, BENRIG COTTAGE and STABLE HOUSE SITUATED ON THE SAME ROAD. Plant stall and cream teas available at Stable House. Parking at Benrig and Mansfield House for all four gardens. St Boswells: 2 minutes from A68 on the A699 to Kelso.
Admission £2.00, includes all gardens.
SUNDAY 30th JUNE 2 - 6 pm
20% to Capability Borders   20% to St Boswells Parish Church

MERTOUN, St Boswells &

(The Duke of Sutherland)

House built by Sir William Scott of Harden in 1703 to the design of Sir William Bruce. Remodelled 1956 by Ian G Lindsay, reducing house to original size. Shrubs, azaleas, redesigned herbaceous borders, ornamental pond, etc. View of the River Tweed. Home made teas. Jedburgh branch British Legion Pipe Band. Plant stall, raffle, cake stall, various other stalls, sideshows etc. St Boswells 2 miles. Driving south on the A68, turn left opposite The Buccleuch Arms Hotel, continue through village and on for about three-quarters of a mile over River Tweed to first Drive on the right.

Admission to garden £1.50 Children under 12 free

SUNDAY 2nd JUNE 2 - 6 pm

40% to Maxton & Mertoun Kirks

MONTEVIOT, Jedburgh

Monteviot stands on a rise above the River Teviot overlooking the rolling Borders countryside. Features include a walled rose garden, shrub and herbaceous borders, water garden of islands linked by bridges, collection of rare trees in pinery.

Rose Day: Jedforest Instrumental Band. Children's activities, including pony rides. Cream teas in house. Stalls including cakes, plants and bottle tombola. Car park free. Dogs on lead. St Boswells 5 miles, Jedburgh 4 miles. Turn off A68 on to B6400 to Nisbet, north of Jedburgh. Entrance second turning on right.

Enquiries to (01835) 830380 9.30am-1pm Monday-Friday.

Admission £2.00 OAPs £1.00 Children under 14 free

SUNDAY 21st JULY (ROSE DAY) 2 - 5 pm

20% to St Mary's Church, Jedburgh
20% to Riding for the Disabled Association, Border Group

STABLE HOUSE, St Boswells &

(Lt Col & Mrs M D Blacklock)

House converted in 1982 and garden started in 1983. "A plant lovers garden. Here, in an informal design, unusual plants are combined with old fashioned roses, shrubs and herbaceous plants to give colour and interest all summer. All in half an acre; also a courtyard garden with tender climbers, small vegetable garden incorporated into mixed border and newly extended gold border."

JOINT OPENING WITH BENRIG, BENRIG COTTAGE AND MANSFIELD HOUSE SITUATED ON THE SAME ROAD.

Home made cream teas in Garden Room and Conservatory. Plant stall. Cake stall and raffle. Parking at Benrig and Mansfield House for all four gardens. St Boswells: two minutes from A68 on the A699 to Kelso.

Admission £2.00, includes all gardens.

SUNDAY 30th JUNE 2 - 6 pm

20% to Capability Borders   20% to St Boswells Parish Church

YETHOLM VILLAGE GARDENS

2 Grafton Court ♿ (Mr G Lee)   **Gladstone House** (Mrs J Hogg)

Ivy House ♿ (Mr & Mrs Patterson)   **4 Morebattle Road** (Mr & Mrs D White)

Grafton House (Mrs J C Baston) Teas only.   **Hill View** (Mr & Mrs Dodds)

Yetholm Village is situated at the foot of the Cheviot Hills. Each garden has its own endearing character and is filled with a variety of herbaceous shrubs, fruit trees and colourful bedding plants. There may be the opportunity to appreciate an organic vegetable garden. Tickets will be sold on the Village Green where there will be a produce stall. Home baked teas at Grafton House and Gladstone House. Ample parking.

Admission £1.50, includes all gardens.

SUNDAY 4th AUGUST 2 - 6pm

20% to Children's Hospice Association Scotland

20% to St Columba's Hospice, Edinburgh

STEWARTRY OF KIRKCUDBRIGHT

District Organiser:	**Mrs M R C Gillespie,** Danevale Park, Crossmichael, Castle Douglas DG7 2LP
Area Organisers:	**Miss P Bain,** Annick Bank, Hardgate, Castle Douglas DG7 3LD
	Mrs C Cathcart, Culraven, Borgue, Kirkcudbright DG6 4SG
	Mrs A Chandler, Auchenvin, Rockcliffe, Dumfries DG5 4QQ
	Mrs Jane Hannay, Kirklandhill, Kirkpatrick Durham, Castle Douglas DG7 3EZ
	Mrs W J McCulloch, Ardwall, Gatehouse of Fleet DG7 2EN
	Mrs C A Ramsay, Limits, St Johns, Dalry, Castle Douglas DG7 3SW
Hon. Treasurer:	**Mr W Little,** 54 St Andrew Street, Castle Douglas DG7 1EN

DATES OF OPENING

Corsock House, Castle Douglas	By appointment	
Danevale Park, Crossmichael	Date to be announced	
Walton Park, Castle Douglas	Sunday 28 April	2 – 5pm
Barnhourie Mill, Colvend	Sunday 26 May	2 – 5pm
Corsock House, Castle Douglas	Sunday 2 June	2 – 5pm
Cally Gardens, Gatehouse of Fleet	Sunday 16 June	10am – 5.30pm
Southwick House, Dalbeattie	Sunday 23 June	2 – 5pm
	& afternoons 24-28 June	
Kirkcudbright Gardens	Sunday 7 July	2 - 5pm
Argrennan House, Castle Douglas	Sunday 14 July	2 – 5pm

Hensol, Mossdale .... Sunday 21 July		2 – 5pm
Threave School of Gardening .... Sunday 4 August		9am-5.30pm
Cally Gardens, Gatehouse of Fleet .... Sunday 11 August		10am – 5.30pm

ARGRENNAN HOUSE, Castle Douglas &

(Robert Reddaway & Tulane Kidd)
Georgian house set in beautiful parkland with specimen trees. A large walled garden with traditional herbaceous borders, shrub borders and rose garden. Water garden with box parterres and 1840 rockery. Woodland walks. Water garden, ponds and bog gardens. Teas served in old kitchen. House not open. Route: Castle Douglas 3½ miles. Kirkcudbright 3½ miles on A711.
Admission £1.50 Children 50p
SUNDAY 14th JULY 2 - 5 pm
40% to Crossroads Care Attendant Scheme (Stewartry branch)

BARNHOURIE MILL, Colvend & (partly)

(Dr M R Paton)
Flowering shrubs and trees, dwarf conifers and an especially fine collection of rhododendron species. Tea in house £1. Cars free. Dalbeattie 5 miles. Route A710 from Dumfries.
Admission £1.50 Children free
SUNDAY 26th MAY 2 - 5pm
Also open by appointment. Tel: 01387 780269
40% to Scottish Wildlife Trust

CALLY GARDENS, Gatehouse of Fleet &

(Mr Michael Wickenden)
A specialist nursery in a fine 2.7 acre, 18th century walled garden with old vinery and bothy, all surrounded by the Cally Oak woods. Our collection of 3,000 varieties can be seen and many will be available pot-grown, especially rare herbaceous perennials. Forestry nature trails nearby. Route: From Dumfries take the Gatehouse turning off A75 and turn left, through the Cally Palace Hotel Gateway from where the gardens are well signposted. Voluntary admission charge
SUNDAYS 16th JUNE and 11th AUGUST 10 am - 5.30 pm
40% to Save the Children Fund

CORSOCK HOUSE, Castle Douglas

(Mr & Mrs M L Ingall)
Rhododendrons, woodland walks with temples , water gardens and loch. David Bryce turretted "Scottish Baronial" house in background. Teas by Corsock WRI. Cars free. Dumfries 14 miles, Castle Douglas 10 miles, Corsock ½ mile on A712.
Admission £1.50 Children 50p
SUNDAY 2nd JUNE 2 - 5 pm
Also open by appointment: Tel. 01644 440250
40% to Gardeners' Royal Benevolent Society

DANEVALE PARK, Crossmichael

(Mrs M R C Gillespie)
Open for snowdrops. Woodland walks. Tea in house. Route: A713. Crossmichael 1 mile, Castle Douglas 3 miles. Admission £1.50
DATE TO BE ANNOUNCED
40% to Crossmichael Village Hall

HENSOL, Mossdale, Castle Douglas ♿
(Lady Henderson)
An early 19th century granite house designed by Lugar. Established garden surrounding house. Alpines, shrubs, water garden and new woodland garden. River walks. Plant stall. Cars free. Tea in house. Route: A762, 3 miles north of Laurieston.
Admission £1.50 Children 50p
SUNDAY 21st JULY 2 - 5 pm
40% to R N L I

#KIRKCUDBRIGHT GARDENS
16 High Street (Mr Robert Mitchell)
19th century town garden. Teas. Plant stall. No dogs please.
Greengate & Close, High Street (Mr & Mrs J M Craig)
Small garden down close in historic High Street conservation area.
Other cottage gardens in the close also open. Trees, shrubs, herbaceous, roses.
Plant stall. No dogs please.
Parking and toilets in Harbour Square whence both gardens a short walk up narrow High Street.
Admission £1.50 Children 50p includes all gardens
SUNDAY 7th JULY 2 - 5pm
40% to Cancer Relief Macmillan Fund

SOUTHWICK HOUSE, Dalbeattie ♿ (formal garden only)
(Mrs C H Thomas)
Formal garden with lily ponds and herbaceous borders, shrubs, vegetables, fruit and greenhouse. Water garden with boating pond, lawns and fine trees, through which flows the Southwick burn. Tea & biscuits, ice cream and soft drinks. On A710, near Caulkerbush. Dalbeattie 7 miles, Dumfries 17 miles.
Admission £1.50 Children 50p
SUNDAY 23rd JUNE 2 - 5 pm, also 24th - 28th June with honesty box
40% to Cancer Relief Macmillan Fund (Dalbeattie & District Committee)

THREAVE SCHOOL OF PRACTICAL GARDENING, Castle Douglas ♿
(The National Trust for Scotland)
Baronial house by Peddie & Kinnear. 60 acres of garden. Ornamental, fruit, vegetable and glasshouses. House not open. Plant stall. Route: A75, one mile west of Castle Douglas.
Admission £3.60 Children & OAPs £2.40
SUNDAY 4th AUGUST 9 am - 5.30 pm
40% to The Gardens Fund of The National Trust for Scotland
For other opening details see page 132

WALTON PARK, Castle Douglas ♿
(Mr Jeremy Brown)
Early 19th century double bow-fronted house with later additions. Walled garden, gentian border. Flowering shrubs, rhododendrons and azaleas. Cars free. Tea in house. Plant stall. Route: B794, 3½ miles from A75.
Admission £1.50 Children 50p
SUNDAY 28th APRIL 2 - 5 pm
40% to Carnsalloch Cheshire Home

TWEEDDALE

District Organiser:	**Mrs John Kennedy,** Hazlieburn, West Linton EH46 7AS
Area Organisers:	**Mrs D Balfour-Scott,** Langlawhill, Broughton, Lanarkshire ML12 6HL
	Mrs R K Brown, Runic Cross, Waverley Road, Innerleithen EH44 6QH
	Mrs H B Marshall, Baddinsgill, West Linton, EH46 7HL
Hon. Treasurer:	**Mr K St C Cunningham,** Hallmanor, Peebles EH45 9JN

DATES OF OPENING

Kailzie Gardens, Peebles .... Daily 23 March – 19 October   11 – 5.30pm
Winter daylight hours, gardens only

Dawyck Botanic Garden .... Sunday 5 May	10am – 6pm
Haystoun, Peebles .... Sunday 26 May	2-5.30pm
Hallmanor, Kirkton Manor .... Sunday 2 June	2 – 6pm
Stobo Water Garden, Stobo .... Sunday 9 June	2 – 6pm
Cringletie House Hotel, Eddleston .... Sat & Sun 29/30 June	2 – 5pm
Portmore, Eddleston .... Sunday 28 July	2 – 5pm

CRINGLETIE HOUSE HOTEL, Eddleston &
(Mr & Mrs S L Maguire)
House by David Bryce. Former home of Wolfe Murray family, set in 28 acres of woodlands, including walled garden which includes fruit trees, vegetables etc. Herbaceous borders. Tea 3.30 - 4.30 pm. Cars free. Peebles 2½ miles. Donation box. Bus: No.62 Edinburgh/Peebles. Hotel signposted from A703 Edinburgh/Peebles. SGS signs.
SATURDAY 29th JUNE 2 - 5 pm
40% to St Columba's Hospice
SUNDAY 30th JUNE 2 - 5 pm
40% to the Royal Blind Asylum

DAWYCK BOTANIC GARDEN, Stobo & (limited access)
(Specialist Garden of the Royal Botanic Garden, Edinburgh)
Arboretum of rare trees, rhododendrons and other shrubs. Terraces and stonework constructed by Italian landscape gardeners in 1820. Free guided tours of spring colour and woodlands throughout the open day. Conservatory shop with plant sales, coffees and teas. Guide dogs only. Route: 8 miles south west of Peebles on B712. SGS signs. Admission £2.00 Concessions £1.50 Children 50p Families £4.50
SUNDAY 5th MAY 10 am - 6 pm
40% to Royal Botanic Garden, Edinburgh
For other opening details see page 141

TWEEDDALE

HALLMANOR, Kirkton Manor, Peebles
(Mr & Mrs K St C Cunningham)
Rhododendrons and azaleas, primulas, wooded grounds with loch and salmon ladder.
800 ft above sea level in the Manor valley. Teas. Plant stall. Peebles 6 miles. Off A72
Peebles/Glasgow road. Follow SGS signs.
Admission £1.50 Children free
SUNDAY 2nd JUNE 2 - 6 pm
40% to Manor & Lyne Church

HAYSTOUN, Peebles   &. (partly)
(Mr & Mrs D Coltman)
16th century house (not open). Walled garden, recently planted wild garden with
newly created ornamental loch which has beautiful walks around it. Teas. Plant stall.
Dogs on lead only please. A703 Edinburgh/Peebles over Tweed bridge in Peebles,
follow SGS signs for 1½ miles.
Admission £1.50 Children free
SUNDAY 26th MAY 2 - 5.30pm
40% to St Columba's Hospice

KAILZIE GARDENS, Peebles &.
(Lady Buchan-Hepburn)
Semi-formal walled garden with rose garden, herbaceous borders and old fashioned
roses. Greenhouses. Woodland and burnside walks among massed spring bulbs and,
later, rhododendrons and azaleas. The gardens, set among fine old trees, lie in the
beautiful Tweed valley with views across to the Border hills. Free car park. Picnic area.
Children's play corner. Home made teas and lunches in licensed restaurant. Art
Gallery. Shop. Plant stalls. Stocked trout pond. Parties by arrangement.
Admission: Summer £2.00, children 5-14 50p Winter £1.00, children 50p
OPEN ALL YEAR ROUND Summer: 23rd March - 19th October 11am - 5.30pm.
Winter: during daylight hours, the gardens only.
Special Snowdrop Days as advertised locally.
Donation to Scotland's Gardens Scheme

PORTMORE, Eddleston
(Mr & Mrs D H L Reid)
Herbaceous borders. Herb garden. Ornamental vegetable garden. Greenhouse with
Victorian grotto. Newly planted shrub rose garden and parterre. Cream teas. Dogs on
lead please. Edinburgh to Peebles bus No.62.
Admission £1.50
SUNDAY 28th JULY 2 - 5 pm
40% to Crossroads Care Attendant Scheme

STOBO WATER GARDEN, Stobo, Peebles
(Mr Hugh Seymour)
Water garden, lakes, azaleas and rhododendrons. Woodland walks. Cars free. Cream
teas in village hall. Peebles 7 miles, signposted on B712 Lyne/Broughton road.
Admission £1.50 Children free
SUNDAY 9th JUNE 2 - 6 pm
20% to Stobo Kirk, 20% to European Aid (Scottish)

WIGTOWN

District Organiser:	**Mrs Francis Brewis,** Ardwell House, Stranraer DG9 9LY
Area Organisers:	**Mrs V Brinton,** Chlenry, Castle Kennedy, Stranraer DG9 8SL
	Mrs Andrew Gladstone, Craichlaw, Kirkcowan, Newton Stewart DG8 0DQ
Hon. Treasurer:	**Mr G S Fleming,** Bank of Scotland, 64 George Street, Stranraer DG9 7JN

DATES OF OPENING

Ardwell House Gardens, Ardwell .... Daily 1 April – 30 September   10am – 5pm

Castle Kennedy & Lochinch Gardens,
   Stranraer .... Daily 1 April – 30 September   10am - 5pm

Glenwhan, Dunragit, Stranraer .... Daily 1 April – 30 September

Whitehills, Newton Stewart .... 1 April – 31 October   by appointment

Logan Botanic Garden, Port Logan .... Sunday 26 May   10am – 6pm
Monreith House Garden, Port William .... Sunday 26 May   10am-5pm
Whitehills, Newton Stewart .... Sunday 2 June   2 – 5pm
Bargaly House, Palnure .... Sunday 16 June   2 – 5pm
New Luce Village Gardens .... Sunday 14 July   2 - 5pm

ARDWELL HOUSE GARDENS, Ardwell, Stranraer
(Mrs Faith Brewis & Mr Francis Brewis)
Daffodils, spring flowers, rhododendrons, flowering shrubs, coloured foliage and rock plants. Moist garden at smaller pond and a walk round larger ponds, with views over Luce Bay. Plants for sale and self-pick fruit in season. Collecting box. House not open. Dogs welcome on leads. Picnic site on shore. Teas available in Ardwell village. Stranraer 10 miles. Route A76 towards Mull of Galloway.
Admission £1.50 Children & OAPs 50p
DAILY 1st APRIL to 30th SEPTEMBER 10 am - 5 pm
Donation to Scotland's Gardens Scheme

BARGALY HOUSE, Palnure, Newton Stewart &
(Mr Jonathan Bradburn)
Unusual trees and shrubs in extensive borders, rock and water garden, walled garden with large herbaceous border. Woodland and river walks. Refreshments available. Palnure 2 miles, A75. Bus stop, Palnure.
Admission £1.50 Children 50p
SUNDAY 16th JUNE 2 - 5 pm
Donation to Scotland's Gardens Scheme

CASTLE KENNEDY & LOCHINCH GARDENS, Stranraer &

(The Earl & Countess of Stair)
The gardens are laid out on a peninsula betwen two lochs and extend to 75 acres from the ruined Castle Kennedy to Lochinch Castle. They are world famous for rhododendrons, azaleas, magnolias and embothriums and contain specimens from Hooker and other expeditions. Choice of peaceful walks. Plant centre. Gift shop with refreshments. Admission charged. 20% discount for parties over 30 people. Cars and disabled free.
Stranraer 5 miles on A75. For further information telephone 01776-702024.
DAILY 1st APRIL - 30th SEPTEMBER   10 am - 5 pm
Donation to Scotland's Gardens Scheme

GLENWHAN, Dunragit, Stranraer &

(Mr & Mrs William Knott)
A hill top garden with splendid views of Luce Bay. Trees, shrubs, rock and water gardens in natural landscape round two lochans. Car park free. No dogs except guide dogs, please. Lunches and refreshments available. Plant stall.
Admission £1.50 Children under 14 50p
Daily APRIL - SEPTEMBER
Donation to Scotland's Gardens Scheme

LOGAN BOTANIC GARDEN, Port Logan, by Stranraer &

(Specialist Garden of the Royal Botanic Garden, Edinburgh)
One of the most exotic gardens in Britain. Magnificent tree ferns and cabbage palms grow within a walled garden together with a rich array of southern hemisphere plants. Licensed Salad Bar and Shop with gifts, crafts and plant sales; open 10am to 6pm. Guide dogs only. Route: 10m south of Stranraer on A716, then 2½ miles from Ardwell village.
Admission £2.00 Concessions £1.50 Children 50p Families £4.50
SUNDAY 26th MAY   10 am - 6 pm
40% to Royal Botanic Garden, Edinburgh
For other opening details see page 140

#MONREITH HOUSE GARDEN, Port William

(Sir Michael Maxwell Bt)
Once famous garden created by Sir Herbert Maxwell, one of the great pioneers of Scottish gardening. It has been neglected for over 50 years, but restoration is just beginning. Interesting trees and shrubs. Teas. 2m from Port William off B7021 Port William/Whithorn.
Admission £2.00 Children & OAPs £1.00 includes entry to House.
SUNDAY 26th MAY   10am - 5pm
40% to Monreith Trust

#NEW LUCE VILLAGE GARDENS

4 or 5 gardens in this small conservation village, ranging from small woodland gardens to the walled gardens of Lucewater House. The Rivers Luce and Crosswater of Luce are interesting features, as is the ruined abbey of Glenluce nearby. Teas in Village Hall.
5m off A75 Dumfries/Stranraer, turning at either Glenluce or Castle Kennedy.
Admission £2.00 Children & OAPs £1.00 includes all gardens.
SUNDAY 14th JULY 2 - 5pm
40% to British Red Cross Society

WHITEHILLS, Newton Stewart &

(Mr & Mrs C A Weston)

Rhododendrons, azaleas, heathers and many exotic shrubs. Scree, water and winter gardens. Woodland walks. Rhododendron and shrub nursery. Plant stall. Tea. Dogs on lead only. Ample parking. Newton Stewart 1 mile. Wood of Cree road ¼ mile north of Minnigaff Church (sign posted to RSPB reserve).

Admission £1.50 Accompanied children under 14 free

SUNDAY 2nd JUNE 2 - 5pm

Open by appointment from 1st April to 31st October. Tel: 01671 402049

40% to Friends of Newton Stewart Hospital

GARDENS OPEN UNDER THE NATIONAL GARDENS SCHEME IN CUMBRIA

DATES OF OPENING

Palace How, Brackenthwaite .... Monday 27 May   11am - 5pm
Hutton-in-the-Forest, Penrith .... Sundays 2 June & 21 July   11am - 5pm
The Mill House, Sebergham .... Sunday 30 June   1.30-4.30pm
38 English Street, Longtown .... Sunday 21 July   2 - 5pm

38 ENGLISH STREET, Longtown, Carlisle

(Mr & Mrs C Thomson)

Terraced house garden. Red sandstone and water features; containers and troughs, pergola and herbaceous. Tea. Plant sale. Route: M6 junction 44, A7 for 6m into Longtown. 300 yards on left, next door to Annes Hairdressers. No dogs please.

Admission £1.00 Children free.

SUNDAY 21st JULY 2 - 5pm.   Private visits welcome: Tel. 01228 791364.

HUTTON-IN-THE-FOREST, Penrith &

(Lord Inglewood)

Magnificent grounds with 18th century walled flower garden, terraces and lake. 19th century low garden, specimen trees and topiary; woodland walk and dovecote. Medieval house with 17th,18th & 19th century additions. Teas. Route: 5m north west of Penrith, 3m from Exit 41 of M6.

Admission £2 gardens & grounds, £3.50 house, gardens & grounds. Children free in gardens & grounds; £1.50 house, gardens & grounds.

Gardens and grounds OPEN DAILY ALL YEAR, except Saturdays, 11am - 5pm.

For National Gardens Scheme **SUNDAYS 2nd JUNE & 21st JULY 11am - 5pm**

PALACE HOW, Brackenthwaite, Loweswater ♿
(Mr & Mrs A & K Johnson)
Established damp garden set in lovely situation amongst mountains. Unusual trees and shrubs, especially rhododendrons and acers. Pond with bog plants; candelabra primulas; Himalayan poppies, roses and alpines. Cream teas at Loweswater Village Hall, in aid of NSPCC. Plant sale. Route: 6m SE of Cockermouth on B5292 and B5289 or from Keswick 10m over Whinlatter Pass, through Lorton village, follow signs for Loweswater. No dogs please.
Admission £1.50 Children free.
MONDAY 27th MAY 11am - 5pm. Private visits welcome: Tel. 01900 85648.

THE MILL HOUSE, Sebergham
(Mr & Mrs R L Jefferson)
$\frac{1}{2}$ acre garden set in secluded valley around water mill; features millstream and pond, large herbaceous border, gravel garden, fruit & vegetable garden. Tea (in aid of Welton School Trust). Plant sale. Route: Junction 41 off M6 Penrith/Wigton road into Sebergham, turning L into easily missed lane just before bridge over R. Caldew, 200yds up lane, after bungalow take L fork in drive. No dogs please. Ample parking.
Admission £1.50 Children free.
SUNDAY 30th JUNE 1.30 - 4.30pm

GARDENS OF SCOTLAND 1997

To: The Director, Scotland's Gardens Scheme
31 Castle Terrace, Edinburgh EH1 2EL

Please send a copy of "Gardens of Scotland" as soon as it is available. I enclose a cheque/PO for £3.25, which includes postage, payable to Scotland's Gardens Scheme.

Name ....

Address ....

....

.... Post Code ....

Edinburgh Butterfly and Insect World.

Whatever the weather, stroll through the wonderful world of an exotic rainforest, a landscape of tropical plants surrounding splashing waterfalls and pools. Enjoy the unique pleasure of watching hundreds of the world's most spectacular and colourful butterflies flying all around you. See their entire life cycle at first-hand and marvel at nature's ingenuity. Enter, also, another fascinating world and observe at close quarters the habits of live scorpions, tarantulas, leaf-cutting ants, stick insects, beetles and other remarkable insects. Plus Gift Shop, Garden Centre, Large Free Car Park, Tearoom.

Edinburgh Butterfly and Insect World.

Located at Dobbies Gardening World
on the Edinburgh City Bypass at the Gilmerton exit.
Open Daily 10am to 5pm. Tel 0131 663 4932.

Friendship

Now we feel part of the Rukba family and this is a great comfort.

Dorothy & Bill Howell

♛ The National Trust for Scotland

GARDENS IN TRUST

THE NATIONAL TRUST FOR SCOTLAND is custodian to some of Scotland's finest gardens, from the world-famous Inverewe and Crathes Castle Gardens to the lesser known such as Inveresk Lodge and Malleny Gardens near Edinburgh.

The Trust's work in conserving this heritage of gardens is greatly enhanced by the enjoyment of them by several hundred thousand visitors each year. Visitors, whether members of the Trust or not, contribute financially to the upkeep of our gardens.

Although Trust gardens are open most days of the year, we also give active support to Scotland's Gardens Scheme, opening our gardens on its behalf on special days during the year. A selection of National Trust for Scotland gardens are described in the following pages.

New gardening course at Threave

Since 1960 Threave Garden has been developed with a dual role, as a horticultural training centre as well as an amenity garden. As a result, its wide plant collection and diverse display areas afford not only interest for the Garden's many visitors but also superb opportunities for its student gardeners to learn the skilled craft techniques they will need to develop their careers.

In August 1996, the NTS School of Practical Gardening, Threave, will begin a new, prestige, one-year course of supervised practical instruction for up to six students, each of whom will be offered a self-catering flat within the newly refurbished Threave House, as well as a substantial bursary. A prospectus for this course can be obtained from The Administrator, Threave Garden, Castle Douglas DG7 1RX.

Since it will continue to produce more trained gardeners than the Trust has vacancies to offer on completion of their course, there is the potential for other amenity gardens—including those which open under Scotland's Gardens Scheme—to benefit from this training course.

Arduaine Garden

Argyll & Bute. On A816, 20 miles from Oban and Lochgilphead

Branklyn Garden

A85, Dundee Road, Perth

THIS ATTRACTIVE plantsman's garden at Arduaine occupies a spectacular site overlooking Loch Melfort. It has a superb collection of rhododendrons and specimen trees. Some of these are of remarkable size.

The early garden was of simple, formal design with shelter belts of mixed woodland. Between 1922 and 1929 this garden was developed. In 1971, brothers Harry and Edmund Wright bought the garden and began restoration and improvement. In 1992 they presented the garden to the Trust.

Open all year, daily 9.30 a.m.—sunset. Admission: adult £2.10, child/concession £1.40, adult party £1.70, child/school party £1.00 (family £5.60).

Free entry for The National Trust for Scotland Members.

ON A PERTH HILLSIDE, looking southward over the Tay, Branklyn has been described as "the finest two acres of private garden in the country". An outstanding collection of plants, particularly of alpines, was made by the late Mr and Mrs John Renton. Mr Renton bequeathed the garden to the Trust with an endowment. The Trust agreed to accept the garden because of its great worth—a decision made possible because of generous assistance from the City of Perth.

Open 1 March to 31 October, daily 9.30 a.m.—sunset. Admission: adult £2.10, child/concession £1.40, adult party £1.70, child/school party £1.00 (family £5.60).

Free entry for The National Trust for Scotland Members.

♥ The National Trust for Scotland

Brodick Castle, Garden and Country Park

Isle of Arran. Ferry from Ardrossan (and Kintyre in summer)

BRODICK CASTLE and its gardens on the Isle of Arran came into the care of the Trust in 1958 following the death of the Duchess of Montrose, whose home it was. She created a woodland garden, considered one of the finest rhododendron gardens in Europe. Plants from Himalaya, Burma and China flourish in the gentle west coast climate and give a continuous display of colour from January to August. The formal garden is 250 years old and has recently been restored as a Victorian garden. A country park was established in 1980 through an agreement between Cunninghame District Council and the Trust.

Special nature trail for disabled. Wheelchairs available. Braille sheets.

Open: Castle, 1 April to 31 October, daily 11.30 – 5 (last admission 4.30). Reception Centre, restaurant and shop (dates as castle), 10 – 5. Garden and Country Park, all year, daily 9.30 – sunset.

GOATFELL: open all year.

Admission: Castle and garden, adult £4.10, child/concession £2.70, adult party £3.30, child/ school party £1.00 (family £10.90). Garden only, adult £2.10, child/concession £1.40, adult party £1.70. Car park free. Ferry from Ardrossan (55 minutes) to Brodick. Connecting bus, pier to castle (2 miles). Ferry enquiries to Caledonian MacBrayne: tel. Gourock (01475) 650100.

Free entry for The National Trust for Scotland Members.

❦ The National Trust for Scotland
Crathes Castle and Garden
Aberdeenshire
On A93, 3 miles east of Banchory and 15 miles west of Aberdeen

THE CASTLE AND ITS GARDENS are situated near Banchory, in a delightful part of Royal Deeside. Formerly Crathes was the home of the late Sir James and Lady Burnett of Leys, whose lifelong interests found expression in the gardens and in one of the best collections of trees and shrubs to be found in Britain. Great yew hedges dating from 1702 surround several of the small gardens of which the garden is composed. Given by the late Sir James Burnett of Leys, Bt, in 1951, together with an endowment. Wheelchair access to garden and grounds, trail for disabled, shop, exhibitions, adventure playground, restaurant and toilets for disabled visitors. Wheelchairs available.

Open: Castle, Visitor Centre, shop, licensed restaurant and plant sales. 1 April to 31 October, daily 11 – 5.30 (last admission to castle 4.45). Other times by appointment only. Garden and grounds, all year, daily 9.30 – sunset.

Admission: Castle, garden and grounds, adult £4.10, child/concession £2.70, adult party £3.30, child/school party £1.00 (family £10.90). Grounds only: Adult £1.60, child/concession £1.00, adult party £1.30, child/school party £1.00. Walled Garden only, adult £1.60, child/ concession £1.00, adult party £1.30, child/school party £1.00.

Enquiries and all bookings: tel: Crathes (01330) 844525.

Free entry for The National Trust for Scotland Members.

♛ The National Trust for Scotland

Culzean Castle, Garden and Country Park

South Ayrshire

A719, 4 miles south-west of Maybole and 12 miles south of Ayr

CULZEAN CASTLE AND COUNTRY PARK is the Trust's most visited property and one of the major tourist attractions in Scotland.

The range of interests and activities at Culzean make it a perfect day out for the family. The Fountain Garden lies in front of Robert Adam's magnificent Castle, with terraces and herbaceous borders reflecting its Georgian elegance.

Scotland's first Country Park, consisting of 563 acres, contains a wealth of interest from shoreline through Deer Park, Swan Pond to mature parklands, gardens, woodland walks and adventure playground. A conservatory has been restored to its former glory as an orangery. Ranger/Naturalists located at the Visitor Centre provide excellent services for visitors including many guided walks. An environmental education service and interpretation programme are based on the Country Park.

The Visitor Centre facilities include a shop, licensed self-service restaurant, introductory exhibition to Culzean, auditorium and information. For disabled—lift in castle, toilets, wheelchairs, induction loop for hard of hearing.

Open: Castle, Visitor Centre, licensed self-service restaurant and shops, 1 April to 31 October, daily 10.30 – 5.30 (last tour 5). Other times by appointment. Country Park, all year, daily 9.30 – sunset.

Admission: Castle, adult £3.50, child/concession £1.80; Country Park, adult £3, child/concession £1.50; adult party £2.50, child/school party £1.25, school coaches £20. Combined ticket, Castle and Country Park, adult £5.50, child/concession £3.00, adult party £4.50, child/school party £2.50.

Enquiries and all party bookings: tel. Kirkoswald (01655) 760269.

Additional charge to non-members at special events in August 1996. Details available from the Principal.

Free entry for The National Trust for Scotland members.

Culross Palace Garden

Fife
Off A985, 12 m west of Forth Road Bridge

I n 1994 the Trust reopened Culross Palace and Garden following three years of restoration. The Palace, built between 1597 and 1611, was not a royal palace but the home of Sir George Bruce, a wealthy merchant and pioneer entrepreneur.

A model seventeenth-century garden created by the Trust shows a selection of the plants which might have been available to Sir George Bruce to support the needs of his household. These include a range of vegetables, culinary and medicinal herbs, soft fruit, ornamental shrubs and herbaceous perennials. Terraced and on a steep slope, the garden is laid out in a series of raised beds. Willow hurdle fences, crude rustic plant-supports and crushed-shell paths add to the period effect.

Open: Palace and garden 1 April to 30 September, daily 11-5 (last admission 4). Admission: combined ticket to Palace, Study and Town House, adult £3.60, child/concession £2.40, adult party £2.90, child/school party £1.90 (family £9.60).

Free entry for The National Trust for Scotland Members.

Falkland Palace Garden

Fife
A912, 11 miles north of Kirkcaldy

T HE ROYAL GARDEN at Falkland Palace in Fife, which the Stuart Kings and Queens of Scotland knew, was restored after the war by the late Keeper, Major Michael Crichton Stuart, M.C., M.A., to a design by Percy Cane. Trees and shrubs and herbaceous borders give a long-lasting display from spring-flowering cherries to the rich autumn colouring of the maples. The greenhouse provides a colourful show during the greater part of the year. Ramp into garden for wheelchairs.

Open: Palace and garden, 1 April to 31 October, Monday – Saturday 11 – 5.30, Sunday 1.30 – 5.30 (last admission to palace 4.30, to garden 5). Town Hall, by appointment only.

Admission: palace and garden, adult £4.10, child/concession £2.70, adult party £3.30, child/school party £1.00 (family £10.90). Garden only, adult £2.10, child/concession £1.00, adult party £1.70, child/school party £1.00. Scots Guards and members of the Scots Guards Association (wearing the Association's badge) admitted free.

Free entry for The National Trust for Scotland Members.

Hill of Tarvit

Fife. Off A916
2½ miles south of Cupar

T HIS MANSION HOUSE and garden were remodelled by Sir Robert Lorimer in 1906 for Mr F. B. Sharp. Although the garden was developed and consequently changed, much of the original Lorimer design for it remains. The garden is still being developed with the object of creating greater interest and colour during the year. Bequeathed in 1949 by Miss E. C. Sharp.

Tearoom and House open: Good Friday to Easter Monday and 1 May to 30 September, daily 1.30 – 5.30, weekends in October, 1.30 – 5.30 (last admission 4.45). Tearoom, same dates, but opens 12.30. Gardens and Grounds, 1 April to 31 October, daily 9.30 – 7; 1 November to 31 March, daily 9.30 – 4.

Admission: house and garden, adult £3.10, child/ concession £2.00, adult party £2.50, child/school party £1.00, (family £8.20), garden only (honesty box), £1.00.

Free entry for The National Trust for Scotland Members.

Inveresk Lodge Garden

East Lothian. A6124 south of Musselburgh, 6 miles east of Edinburgh

I NVERESK, on the southern fringes of Musselburgh, is one of the most unspoiled villages of the Lothians. The 17th century Lodge (which is not open to the public) is the oldest building in the village. The garden has been almost completely remodelled since the Trust was presented with the property and an endowment, by Mrs Helen E. Brunton in 1959. This reconstruction is rather similar to the garden as it was in 1851. This is a happy coincidence, for the old plan was found after the present layout was completed. There are good examples of shrubs, trees and other plants for smaller gardens

Open: 1 April to 30 September, Monday – Friday 10 – 4.30, Saturday/Sunday 2 – 5, 1 October to 31 March, Monday – Friday 10 – 4.30, Sunday 2 – 5.

Admission: £1.00 (honesty box).

Free entry for The National Trust for Scotland Members.

❦ The National Trust for Scotland
Inverewe Garden
Highland
On A832, by Poolewe, 6 miles north-east of Gairloch

THIS MAGNIFICENT HIGHLAND GARDEN, near Poolewe, is in an impressive setting of mountains, moorland and sea-loch and attracts over 130,000 visitors a year. When it was founded in 1862 by Osgood Mackenzie, only a dwarf willow grew where plants from many lands now flourish in a profusion as impressive as it is unexpected. Planned as a wild garden it includes Australian tree ferns, exotic plants from China, and a magnificent *Magnolia campbellii*. Given into the care of the Trust in 1952 by Mrs Mairi T. Sawyer, together with an endowment. Disabled access to greenhouse and half paths. Wheelchairs available. Toilets.

Open: garden, 1 April to 31 October, daily 9.30 – 9, 1 November to 31 March, daily 9.30 – 5. Visitor Centre and shop, 1 April to 31 October, daily 9.30 – 5.30. Licensed restaurant, same dates, daily 10 – 5. Guided garden walks with gardener, 1 April to 31 October, Monday to Friday at 1.30.

Admission: Adult £3.60, child/concession £2.40, adult party £2.90, child/school party £1.00 (family £9.60).

Free entry for The National Trust for Scotland Members.

Kellie Castle Garden

Fife

On B9171, 3 miles north north-west of Pittenweem

A GARDEN made by Sir Robert Lorimer and subsequently restored by the Trust. Professor James Lorimer, Sir Robert's father, restored and made his home at Kellie Castle near Pittenweem, Fife. A delightful model of a late Victorian garden with box edged paths, rose arches, many period roses, herbaceous plants, soft and tree fruits and a collection of interesting old-fashioned vegetables. The castle is a fine example of the domestic architecture of the Lowland counties of Scotland in the 16th and 17th centuries. Video programme. Tearoom. Wheelchair access to garden. Induction loop for the hard of hearing.

Open: Castle, Good Friday to Easter Monday and 1 May to 30 September, daily 1.30 – 5.30; weekends in October 1.30 – 5.30 (last admission 4.45). Garden and grounds, 1 April to 31 October, daily 9.30 – 7; 1 November to 31 March, daily 9.30 – 4.

Admission: Castle and garden, adult £3.60, child/ concession £2.40, adult party £2.90, child/school party £1.00 (family £9.60).

Free entry for The National Trust for Scotland Members

Leith Hall Garden

Aberdeenshire. On B9002,
1 mile west of Kennethmont and
34 miles north-west of Aberdeen

THIS ATTRACTIVE old country house at Kennethmont, Aberdeenshire, the earliest part of which dates from 1650, was the home of the Leith and Leith-Hay families for more than three centuries. Exhibition on the Military Lairds of Leith Hall, entitled "For Crown and Country". Picnic area. The west garden was made by Mr and The Hon. Mrs Charles Leith-Hay around the beginning of the present century. The rock garden has recently been enhanced by The Scottish Rock Garden Club in celebration of their 150th anniversary. Mr and Mrs Charles Leith-Hay also improved the garden, and instituted many other improvements to the policies. Their work was later continued by Mrs Leith-Hay's niece and her husband, Col. and Mrs Derrick Gascoigne. The property was given to the Trust by The Hon. Mrs Leith-Hay in 1945. Toilet for disabled.

Open: house and tearoom, Good Friday to Easter Monday and 1 May to 30 September, daily 1.30 – 5.30; weekends in October, 1.30 – 5.30 (last admission 4.45). Garden and grounds, all year, daily 9.30 – sunset.

Admission: house, adult £3.60, child/concession £2.40, adult party £2.90, child/school party £1.00 (family £9.60). Garden and grounds, adult £1.60, child/concession £1.00, adult party £1.30, child/school party £1.00.

Free entry for The National Trust for Scotland Members

Priorwood Garden

Borders
A6091, in Melrose

THIS SMALL FORMAL GARDEN specialising in flowers for drying is situated in the middle of Melrose, Borders, adjacent to Melrose Abbey. Features include herbaceous border and beds of annual flowers suitable for drying. A wide range of information and drying aids, together with dried flowers from the garden, are on sale. Orchard walk. The property was purchased by the Trust in 1974.

Garden, NTS Shop and Dried-Flower Shop Open: 1 April to 30 June, and 1 to 30 September, Monday – Saturday 10 – 5.30, Sunday 1.30 – 5.30. 1 July to 31 August, Monday – Saturday 10 – 6.30, Sunday 1.30 – 6.30, 1 October to 24 December, Monday – Saturday 10 – 4, Sunday 1.30 – 4. NTS Shop, 9 January to 31 March, Monday – Saturday 12 – 4; 1 April to 24 December, Monday – Saturday 10 – 5.30, Sunday 1.30 – 5.30 (closed 28 October to 5 November for stocktaking).

Admission: £1.00 (honesty box).

Best seen June to October.

Free entry for The National Trust for Scotland Members.

Pitmedden Garden

**Aberdeenshire. On A920, 1 mile west of
Pitmedden village and 14 miles north of Aberdeen**

AT PITMEDDEN, near Udny, Aberdeenshire, the National Trust for Scotland has re-created the 17th-century "Great Garden" originally laid out by Sir Alexander Seton, the first baronet of Pitmedden. Given to the Trust with an endowment from the late Major James Keith in 1951 and under the guidance of Dr James Richardson H.R.S.A., the formal parterres were re-created. Three of them derive from designs possibly used at Holyrood in Edinburgh and a fourth is a tribute to the Setons, using the family crest and Scottish Heraldry. Fountains and sundials make excellent centrepieces to the garden filled with 40,000 annual flowers. The Museum of Farming Life from its formation in 1980 has now grown to become one of the best exhibitions of Farming Life in the north-east. Extensive herbaceous borders, fruit trees and Herb Garden. Facilities for the disabled. Garden Room. Tearoom. Visitor Centre. Shop. Guided Tours available.

Open: Garden, Visitor Centre, museum, grounds and other facilities, 1 May to 30 September, daily 10 – 5.30 (last tour 5).

Admission: Garden and museum, adult £3.10, child/concession £2.00, adult party £2.50, child/school party £1.00 (family £8.20).

Free entry for The National Trust for Scotland Members.

♥ The National Trust for Scotland
Threave Garden
Dumfries and Galloway
Off A75, 1 mile west of Castle Douglas

THIS VICTORIAN MANSION HOUSE near Castle Douglas, Dumfries and Galloway Region, with policies, woodland and gardens extending in all to 1,490 acres, was presented to the Trust with an endowment in 1947 by the late Major A. F. Gordon of Threave. In 1960 the house was adapted for use for a school of horticulture, giving particular emphasis to practical training within the 60-acre gardens. A diverse amenity garden with an outstanding plant collection has been developed since then.

Open: Garden, all year, daily 9.30 – sunset. Walled garden and glasshouses, all year, daily 9.30 – 5. Visitor Centre, exhibition and shop, 1 April to 31 October, daily 9.30 – 5.30. Restaurant, 10 – 5.

Admission: adult £3.60, child/concession £2.40, adult party £2.90, child/school party £1.00 (family £9.60).

Free entry for The National Trust for Scotland Members.

HEAD GARDENERS' MEETING

The National Trust for Scotland arranges an annual meeting of Head Gardeners from Trust and privately owned gardens. The objects are to enable gardeners to maintain contact with others in their profession and to keep up to date with recent technical developments, and to allow visits to be made to local gardens or nurseries of interest. Meetings are normally based in a hall of residence.

Owners or staff from gardens which are open under Scotland's Gardens Scheme are welcome to apply for one of the limited places available. Please ask for further details from the Gardens Department, The National Trust for Scotland, 5 Charlotte Square, Edinburgh EH2 4DU, (telephone (0131) 226 5922).

♥ The National Trust for Scotland
OTHER TRUST GARDEN PROPERTIES
(Free entry for The National Trust for Scotland Members)

BRODIE CASTLE, MORAY
A garden being restored to include a selection of the Brodie collection of daffodils and other varieties. Interesting mature trees and avenue. Open: castle, 1 Apr (or Good Friday if earlier) to 30 Sep, Mon-Sat 11-5.30, Sun 1.30-5.30; weekends in Oct, Sat 11-5.30, Sun 1.30-5.30 (last admission 4.30). Other times by appointment. Grounds, all year, daily 9.30 sunset.
Admission: adult £3.60, child/concession £2.40; adult party £2.90, child/ school party £1.00, family £9.60. Grounds only (outwith summer season's published opening times): £1 (honesty box).

BROUGHTON HOUSE, KIRKCUDBRIGHT, DUMFRIES AND GALLOWAY
A charming one-acre garden created by the artist E.A. Hornel between 1901 and 1933, which includes a 'Japanese-style' garden influenced by his many visits to the Far East. The garden includes many fine shrubs and herbaceous perennials. Open: house and garden, 1 Apr (or Good Friday if earlier) to 31 Oct, daily 1-5.30.
Admission: adult £2.10, child/concession £1.40; adult party £1.70, child/school party £1, family £5.60.

CASTLE FRASER, ABERDEENSHIRE
A landscaped park with good trees and a walled garden which has been redesigned in a formal manner. Open: castle, Good Friday to Easter Monday, 1 May to 30 Jun and 1 to 30 Sep, daily 1.30-5.30; 1 July to 31 Aug, daily 11-5.30; weekends in Oct, 1.30-5.30 (last admission 4.45). Tearoom, dates as castle, but opens 12.15 in Sep. Garden, all year, daily 9.30-6; grounds, all year, daily 9.30-sunset.
Admission: castle, adult £3.60, child/concession £2.40; adult party £2.90, child/school party £1, family £9.60. Garden and grounds, adult £1.60, child/concession £1; adult party £1.30, child/school party £1.

DRUM CASTLE, ABERDEENSHIRE
Interesting parkland containing a fascinating collection of trees, 100 acre Wood of Drum, Arboretum and Garden of Historic Roses. Open: castle, Good Friday to Easter Monday and 1 May to 30 Sep, daily 1.30-5.30; weekends in Oct, 1.30-5.30 (last admission 4.45). Garden, same dates, daily 10-6. Grounds, all year, daily 9.30 sunset.
Admission: castle, garden and grounds, adult £3.60, child/concession £2.40; adult party £2.90, child/school party £1, family £9.60. Garden and grounds only, adult £1.60, child/concession £1; adult party £1.30, child/school party £1.

GREENBANK GARDEN, CLARKSTON, GLASGOW
A Gardening Advice Centre offering a series of regular guided walks. Garden with an excellent collection of shrub roses. Programme of events available on request. Special garden for the disabled. Open: all year, daily 9.30-sunset, except 25/26 Dec and 1/2 Jan. Shop and tearoom, 1 Apr (or Good Friday if earlier) to 31 Oct, daily 11-5. House open 1 Apr to 31 Oct, Sundays only, 2-4 (subject to functions in progress).
Admission: adult £2.60, child/concession £1.70; adult party £2.10, child/school party £1, family £6.90. No dogs in garden, please.

THE HILL HOUSE, HELENSBURGH
The garden at The Hill House complements the finest example of the domestic architecture of Charles Rennie Mackintosh and is being restored to represent the designs of Walter Blackie with features by Mackintosh.Open: 1 Apr (or Good Friday if earlier) to 31 Oct, daily 1.30-5.30 (last admission 5); tearoom, 1.30-4.30.
Admission: adult £3.60, child/concession £2.40; adult party £2.90, child/school party £1, family £9.60.

HOUSE OF DUN, MONTROSE, ANGUS
Restoration of the gardens is based largely on designs originally conceived by Lady Augusta FitzClarence using typical plants of the 1840s. Upgrading of the woodlands and their former footpaths is also being carried out. Open: house and shop, Good Friday to Easter Monday and 1 May to 30 Sep, daily 1.30-5.30; weekends in Oct, 1.30-5.30 (last admission 5). Restaurant, same dates, but opens 12.30. Garden and grounds, all year, daily 9.30-sunset.
Admission: house, adult £3.10, child/concession £2; adult party £2.50, child/school party £1, family £8.20. Gardens and grounds only, £1 (honesty box).

MALLENY GARDEN, BALERNO, EDINBURGH
This 17th-century house (not open to the public) has a delightfully personal garden with many interesting plants and features, and a particularly good collection of shrub roses. National Bonsai Collection for Scotland. Open: garden, 1 Apr to 31 Oct, daily 9.30-7; 1 Nov to 31 Mar, daily 9.30-4. House not open.
Admission: £1 (honesty box).

LOCHALSH WOODLAND GARDEN, BALMACARA, HIGHLAND
The woodland garden around Lochalsh House was begun in 1979 following successful experimental rhododendron plantings by E.H.M. Cox in the 1950s; these are complemented by collections of hardy ferns, hydrangeas, fuchsias and *Arundinaria* bamboos. Open all year, daily 9 – sunset. Admission: £1.00 (honesty box).

♛ The National Trust for Scotland
26 Beautiful Gardens to Visit

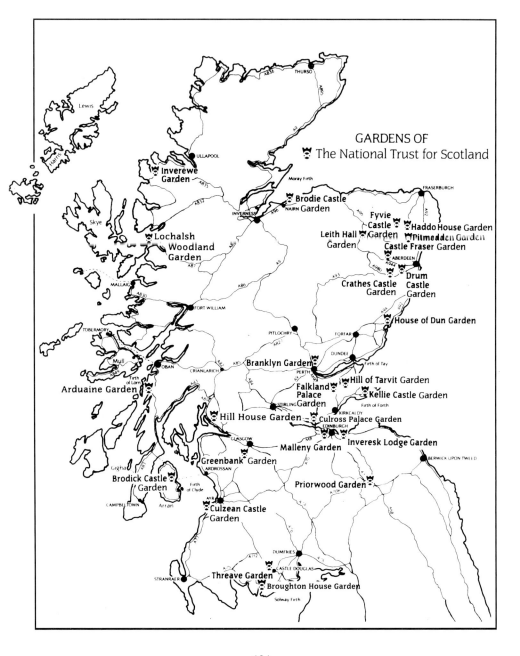

GARDENS OF
♛ The National Trust for Scotland

☙ The National Trust for Scotland
All that we do, we do for you

THE NATIONAL TRUST FOR SCOTLAND belongs to you—to the people who love Scotland—and opens its properties for the enjoyment of all. That's why the brooding magnificence of Glencoe, the soaring mountains of Kintail, the peaceful beaches of Iona and so many great gardens are there for all to see and enjoy, protected for posterity.

At Inverewe Garden, palm trees grow on the same latitude as Labrador. In Brodick Castle Garden the rhododendrons win prizes at flower shows on both sides of the Atlantic. And at The NTS School of Practical Gardening, Threave, we train the head gardeners of the future.

At Culzean Castle, Robert Adam's masterpiece overlooking the Clyde, the stonework is eroded by time and needs continual restoration. Repairs to the viaduct, and many other buildings on the estate now in progress, will take a team of stonemasons several years to complete. And the contents of our properties require as much attention and painstaking care as the exteriors. The Trust has its own bookbinding, metalwork, picture-framing and furniture restoration workshops.

But maintaining properties costs money. Gardens need replanting, curtains frayed with age require to be repaired, and paths on mountains worn by feet need re-seeding. We repair leaky roofs, antiquated plumbing and rusting suits of armour. The list is endless. Each year it costs the Trust almost £14m to carry out this work, quite apart from any new projects we may wish to undertake. That's why we need your help.

If you love the countryside and have a special place in your heart for Scotland, you can help its preservation by joining The National Trust for Scotland. On the next page you will find another six good reasons for joining.

☙ The National Trust for Scotland

Benefits of Membership

WE DON'T ASK FOR MUCH: we believe that we give so much in return. For example the cost of a single membership for a 12-month period is $24.00 and a whole family can join for $40.00—less than an average family night out.

In exchange we give you:

1 Free admission to over 100 properties in Scotland, plus over 300 properties of The National Trust, a completely separate organisation, in England, Wales and Northern Ireland.

2 Our quarterly colour magazine, *Heritage Scotland*, with lists of events, winter activities and a host of opportunities for you to enjoy.

3 Details of our Cruises, Guided Walks and Ranger/Naturalist programmes. And, for those who would like to do a little more, details of how to join one of our Members' support groups.

4 Priority booking for our holiday cottages, and an opportunity to book for our adventure base camps for groups, St Kilda work parties, and Thistle Camps for young people .

5 Our annual illustrated *Guide to Over 100 Properties* listing opening times and facilities.

6 Facilities at our properties for all the family—grandparents, parents and children—including shops with our specially designed range of goods—and tearooms when you need to take the weight off your feet.

The National Trust for Scotland is a charity, independent of Government, supported by 234,000 members

JOIN Scotland's leading conservation organisation

Membership Enrolment Form   Rates valid until 31 October 1996

- ☐ Ordinary: $24.00 or more per annum.
- ☐ Family: $40.00 or more per annum. Two adults at one address (and any of their children, under 18).
- ☐ Life: $480.00 or more (includes cardholder's children under 18).
- ☐ Junior: *$10.00 or more per annum (23 yrs and under).   Date of birth __/__/__

Pensioners: (over 60 and retired) may join at concessionary rates as
Ordinary members $15.00*   ☐
Family members $24.00*   ☐
Life members $240.00   ☐

*Concessionary annual rates are not available to overseas residents.

I enclose remittance for/please charge my Credit Card $_____ Expiry date __/__

Visa/Access/American
Express/Switch No: ☐☐☐☐☐☐☐☐☐☐☐☐☐☐☐☐

Please print

Mr/Mrs/Miss/Ms Surname_____Initials_____

Address:_____

_____

_____Postcode:_____

FOR NTS USE ONLY		
MEMBERSHIP NO.		
TYPE	SOURCE	
	214	
DAY	MONTH	YEAR
Amount received		
$		

Please send to: Membership Services, The National Trust for Scotland, 5 Charlotte Square, Edinburgh EH2 4DU

ROYAL BOTANIC GARDEN
EDINBURGH

One of the world's great
botanical institutions – an
internationally renowned
centre for plant science
research, education and
conservation, whose
unique living collections
are displayed for visitors
in four remarkable
gardens at Edinburgh,
Benmore, Logan
and Dawyck

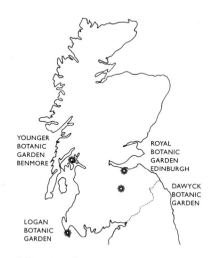

YOUNGER
BOTANIC
GARDEN
BENMORE

ROYAL
BOTANIC
GARDEN
EDINBURGH

DAWYCK
BOTANIC
GARDEN

LOGAN
BOTANIC
GARDEN

For information contact:- The Press Office, Royal Botanic Garden Edinburgh,
20a, Inverleith Row, Edinburgh EH3 5LR, Scotland, U.K.
Tel 0131 552 7171, Direct line 0131 459 0446 ext 427, Fax 0131 552 0382.

FRIENDS OF THE
ROYAL BOTANIC GARDEN EDINBURGH

The Friends organisation was founded in 1991 to support the Garden by taking an active interest in its work. The Friends receive a regular newsletter and can participate in a lively programme of lectures, guided walks, garden visits and plant sales. They have already made valuable contributions towards Garden plant-collecting expeditions and visitor developments.

You too can join in the great tradition of the Garden! Join the Friends! The subscription is £15, or £20 for a family, per annum.

COME TO THE FRIENDS' PLANT SALE • SUNDAY 9 JUNE • 2.30 – 5PM
AT THE GARDEN NURSERY, INVERLEITH AVENUE SOUTH • ALL WELCOME

For information please write or call the Friends Office
Royal Botanic Garden Edinburgh EH3 5LR. Tel 0131 552 5339.

ROYAL BOTANIC GARDEN EDINBURGH

Inverleith Row, Edinburgh

Lothian. Off A902, 1mile north of city centre.

Enjoy one of the world's great gardens; exotic, bizarre and beautiful plants in over 70 acres of superbly landscaped grounds, including the world-famous Rock Garden, the Peat and Woodland Gardens and a tranquil Arboretum. The Glasshouse Experience, a range of ten plant houses, comprises different vegetation zones that reach their climax in Britain's tallest Palm House.

Botanics Shop for gifts, cards, books and plants
Licensed Terrace Cafe and Dill's Snack Bar for meals and light refreshments

OPEN EVERY DAY (except 25 December and 1 January)
ADMISSION FREE, DONATIONS WELCOME

November – February	10am – 4pm
March – April	10am – 6pm
May – August	10am – 8pm
September – October	10am – 6pm

**ROYAL BOTANIC GARDEN EDINBURGH, 20A INVERLEITH ROW,
EDINBURGH EH3 5LR • Tel 0131 552 7171 • Fax 0131 552 0382**

YOUNGER BOTANIC GARDEN BENMORE

Specialist Garden of the Royal Botanic Garden Edinburgh

Argyll. On A815, 7 miles north of Dunoon.

Located in a mountainous landscape on the Cowal peninsula, Benmore is world famous for its extensive range of flowering trees and shrubs, including hundreds of rhododendron species and a remarkable collection of conifers. From a spectacular avenue of Giant Redwoods planted in 1863, numerous waymarked walks lead the visitor, via the formal garden, through hillside woodlands to a viewpoint overlooking the Eachaig valley.

Licensed James Duncan Cafe and Botanics Shop with gifts and plants

Garden open daily, 15 March to 31 October inclusive, 10am to 6pm
(and at other times by arrangement)

Admission £2.00 adults, £1.50 concessions, 50p children, £4.50 families
(Season tickets available at only 3 times day price)

Special Scotland's Gardens Scheme Opening
Admission as above (60% to SGS)

SUNDAY 28 APRIL 10am to 6pm. Free Guided Tours

YOUNGER BOTANIC GARDEN BENMORE, DUNOON, ARGYLL PA23 8QU
Telephone 01369 706261 · Fax 01369 706369

LOGAN BOTANIC GARDEN

Specialist Garden of the Royal Botanic Garden Edinburgh

Wigtownshire. On B7065, 14 miles south of Stranraer.

Located in the extreme south-west of Scotland, virtually surrounded by the sea, Logan is one of the most exotic gardens in Britain. Basking in an exceptionally mild climate, an array of southern hemisphere plants flourish out-of-doors in the setting of an old walled garden, which today contains tree ferns, cabbage palms and chusan palms alongside unusual flowering shrubs, climbers and tender perennials.

Licensed Salad Bar and Botanics Shop with gifts, crafts and plants

Garden open daily, 15 March to 31 October inclusive, 10am to 6pm (and at other times by arrangement)

Admission £2.00 adults, £1.50 concessions, 50p children, £4.50 families (Season tickets available at only 3 times day price)

Special Scotland's Gardens Scheme Opening
Admission as above (60% to SGS)

SUNDAY 26 MAY 10am to 6pm

LOGAN BOTANIC GARDEN, PORT LOGAN, WIGTOWNSHIRE DG9 9ND
Tel 01776 860231 · Fax 01776 860333

DAWYCK BOTANIC GARDEN

Specialist Garden of the Royal Botanic Garden Edinburgh

Tweeddale. On B712, 8 miles south-west of Peebles.

Located in a Borders glen near Stobo, Tweeddale, Dawyck has a history of tree planting stretching back over 300 years. An impressive collection of mature specimen trees, some over 40 metres tall, provide an imposing setting for a variety of flowering trees, shrubs, and herbaceous plants. Landscaped burnside walks, with feature stonework, lead the visitor through mature woodland rich in native flora and fauna.

Conservatory Shop with light refreshments, gifts and plants

Garden open daily, 15 March to 22 October inclusive, 10am to 6pm (and at other times by arrangement)

Admission £2.00 adults, £1.50 concessions, 50p children, £4.50 families (Season tickets available at only 3 times day price)

Special Scotland's Gardens Scheme Opening
Admission as above (60% to SGS)
SUNDAY 5 MAY 10am to 6pm. Free Guided Tours

DAWYCK BOTANIC GARDEN, STOBO, PEEBLESSHIRE EH45 9JU
Tel 01721 760254 · Fax 01721 760214

141

DRUMMOND CASTLE GARDENS, PERTHSHIRE

Scotland's most important formal gardens, among the finest in Europe. The upper terraces offer stunning views and overlook a magnificent parterre celebrating the saltire, family heraldry and the famous multiplex sundial by John Milne, Master Mason to Charles I.

OPEN EASTER WEEKEND, THEN DAILY MAY 1ST TO OCTOBER 31ST 2PM - 6PM (LAST ENTRY 5PM).

Coach party and wheelchair access by arrangement.

Tel: 01764 681257   Fax: 01764 681550

Entrance 2 miles south of Crieff on A822.

Featured recently in United Artists' "Rob Roy"

The Gardeners' Royal Benevolent Society

The Gardeners' Royal Benevolent Society is a charitable organisation which has been helping retired gardeners and their spouses for more than 150 years.

Today it gives assistance to some 500 beneficiaries in the form of sheltered accommodation, quarterly payments, special needs grants, equipment, holidays, support and advice. In Scotland, the Society offers sheltered housing at Netherbyres near Eyemouth in Berwickshire.

FUNDS ARE NEEDED FOR THE SOCIETY'S WORK. You can help by giving a donation or remembering the GRBS in your will and by shopping from GRBS Enterprises Christmas catalogue. When you visit a garden in the *Gardens of Scotland* handbook, you are also contributing to the Society's funds.

APPLICATIONS ARE INVITED FROM RETIRED GARDENERS AND THEIR SPOUSES INTERESTED IN BECOMING BENEFICIARIES.

For further information please contact: Colin Bunce, Chief Executive, The Gardeners' Royal Benevolent Society, Bridge House, 139 Kingston Road, Leatherhead, Surrey KT22 7NT. Telephone: 01372 373962. Fax: 01372 362575.

142

Clan Donald Visitor Centre
Isle of Skye

The **'Garden of Skye'** nestles in a sheltered corner of Skye's Sleat peninsula. The forty acres of woodland garden are based around a 19th century collection of exotic trees. Much of the garden has been restored, displaying plants from around the world. New features include the ponds, rockery, herbaceous borders and a terrace walk.

Within the restored section of Armadale Castle the history of Clan Donald is told in exhibition and audio visual. There are also seasonal exhibitions. Our Countryside Ranger service offers regular events including children's workshops and guided walks.

The Restaurant offers an all day menu and our gift shops have an interesting selection of gifts and books.

Stay for a short break in our self catering cottages and explore the Estate, enjoying the surrounding shoreline and moorland.

Open

Gardens are open all year.

Visitor Centre open every day April to end October 9.30am - 5pm.

Most garden paths and Visitor Centre facilities accessible by wheelchair. Wheelchairs can also be borrowed for use around the Centre.

An induction loop is installed in the video presentation.

Find us

Half a mile north of Armadale ferry port and 14 miles south of Broadford.

HOLIDAYS

Brightwater Holidays are Scotland's specialist Garden Tour Operators. Our fully inclusive itineraries combine the famous and grand gardens with small and private gardens - most tours also visit specialist nurseries. Travel by comfortable coach from a variety of local pick-up points throughout Scotland and the UK. For 1996 we have a variety of garden tours including:

Highland and Island Gardens

Gardens of the Far North (including the Castle of Mey)

The Chelsea Flower Show

Monets' Garden and Gardens of Normandy

Tresco and Cornish Gardens

Norfolks' Lavender Harvest

Dutch Bulbfields Cruise

Homes and Gardens of the Scottish Borders
(including the Gardens of Aikwood Tower -Sir David Steel MP)

Tours commence in early spring when the rhododendrons and azaleas are in bloom, and continue through the summer when herbaceous borders are a kaleidoscope of colour through to autumn when the golds, reds and yellows have that 'Midas Touch'.

Brightwater Holidays
Eden Park House, Cupar, Fife KY15 4HS
Tel: 01334 657155 Fax: 01334 657144

ABTOT No. 5001 - A fully bonded tour operator for your financial protection

David Michie, "Some Poppies at Dawyck" (*Meconopsis sheldonii*), Oil on Canvas, 1995.

Scotland's Gardens Scheme

SUMMER EXHIBITION

11 May - 2 June 1996

10am - 5pm, every day, admission free

Inverleith House, Royal Botanic Garden Edinburgh

Scotland's Gardens Scheme in association with the Royal Botanic Garden Edinburgh, has for the first time invited some of Scotland's best-known artists to take part in a Summer exhibition. Over 50 artists have each chosen to represent one of the Scheme's gardens. The results can be seen at Inverleith House, the award-winning gallery in Edinburgh's Royal Botanic Garden. Paintings will be for sale, with a percentage being donated to Scotland's Gardens Scheme. For details please contact Robin St.Clair-Ford, 31 Castle Terrace, Edinburgh EH1 2EL. Telephone 0131 229 1870. Facsimile 0131 229 0443.

SUPPORTED BY

All is well
in the garden
if you bank with
Adam & Company

The Complete Private Banking Service

THE BUCCLEUCH ESTATES
invite you to visit

BOWHILL HOUSE & COUNTRY PARK, Nr Selkirk (Scottish Borders)

18/19th century house in beautiful countryside. Outstanding art collection, fine French furniture and relics of Duke of Monmouth, Sir Walter Scott and Queen Victoria.

Exciting Adventure Woodland Play Area. Visitor Centre. Nature Trails. Picnic Areas. Mountain Bicycle Hire (01721 20336). Restored Victorian Kitchen. Audio-Visual. Tea Room. Gift Shop.

OPEN 1996

House	1-31 July daily 1-4.30
Country Park	27 April to late Summer Bank Holiday (UK) daily except Fridays 12-5. Open on Fridays during July with House.
Telephone No.	Selkirk (01750) 22204

Off A708—St. Mary's Loch-Moffat Road 3 miles west of Selkirk. Edinburgh 42 miles, Glasgow 75 miles, Berwick 43 miles, Newcastle 80 miles, Carlisle 56 miles.

Bowhill House

DRUMLANRIG CASTLE GARDENS & COUNTRY PARK Nr Thornhill, Dumfriesshire (South-west Scotland)

Castle built 1679-91 on a 15th century Douglas stronghold. Set in parkland ringed by wild hills. French furniture. Paintings by Rembrandt, Holbein and Leonardo. Bonnie Prince Charlie relics. Gift shop. Tea Room.
Exciting Adventure Woodland Play Area. Picnic Sites. Nature Trails. Birds of Prey Centre. Visitors Centre. Craft Centre.

OPEN 1996

Castle and Country Park	Saturday 27 April to Monday 26 August Daily 11 - 5
	Castle closed Thursdays, last entry 4.15pm.
Telephone:	(01848) 330248 - Castle
	(01848) 331555 - Country Park

Off A76, 4 miles north of Thornhill. Glasgow 56 miles, Dumfries 18 miles, Edinburgh 56 miles, Carlisle 51 miles.

Drumlanrig Castle

BOUGHTON HOUSE, Nr Kettering (Northamptonshire)

Northamptonshire home of the Dukes of Buccleuch and their Montagu ancestors since 1528. Important art collection, French and English Furniture and Tapestries. "A vision of Louis XIV's Versailles transported to England".

Exciting Adventure Woodland Play Area. Nature Trail. Tea Room. Gift Shop. Garden Centre.

OPEN 1996

Grounds	1st May-15th September, 1-5 daily, except Fridays.
House and Grounds	1 August-1 September, 2-5 daily. (Grounds open 1 p.m.).
Telephone No.	Kettering (01536) 515731.

Off A43, 3 miles north of Kettering. Northampton 17 miles, Cambridge 45 miles, Coventry 44 miles, Peterborough 32 miles, Leicester 26 miles, London 50 minutes by train.

Boughton House

DALKEITH PARK, Nr Edinburgh (Lothian Region)

Dalkeith Palace not open to public

Nature Trails. Woodland and riverside walks in the extensive grounds of Dalkeith Palace. Tunnel Walk. Adam Bridge. Fascinating Architecture. Exciting Adventure Woodland Play Area. Picnic Area. Barbecue facilities. Information Centre. Scottish farm animals. Ranger service. Come to our new Cafeteria/Shop in our restored Adam stable.

OPEN 1996

Grounds	26 March-29 October, 10 am-6 pm daily.
Telephone Nos.	0131-663 5684 or 0131-665 3277.

Access from east end of Dalkeith High Street.

Off A68, 3 miles from Edinburgh City Boundary.

Dalkeith Palace from the Nature Trail

Parties welcome at all these estates (Special terms and extended opening times for pre-booked parties over 20).
All the houses have special facilities for wheelchair visitors.

148

Torosay Castle
Craignure, Isle of Mull
Telephone: 01680 812421

Torosay is a beautiful family home, designed by eminent architect David Bryce in 1858.

It is surrounded by 12 acres of spectacular gardens, including formal terraces (attributed to Sir Robert Lorimer) and impressive statue walk. Woodland and water gardens, Eucalyptus walk, Japanese garden and rockery, all combine to produce a fine setting for many interesting and tender plants such as Acacia dealbata and Cornus capitata. This splendid garden is offset by spectacular views past Duart Castle and the Sound of Mull to the mountains of Appin and Lorne.

To complete your day out why not take a scenic trip on the Mull Narrow Gauge Railway, a unique way to travel from Craignure to Torosay, and visit the Isle of Mull Weavers, where you can watch craftsmen at work.

Castle & Gardens open mid April to mid October, 10.30am-5pm.
Gardens open all year.

Tearoom, craft/souvenir shop and partial access for the disabled.
Guided tours are available for groups by arrangement.
It's never been easier to get here:
Caledonian MacBrayne ferry Oban/Craignure, then by train, car, Forest Walk (1$^1/_2$ miles)
or by ferry Lochaline-Fishnish (7 miles)
or by motor launch 'Maid of the Firth' from Oban Esplanade, for a short visit.

Telephone or write for further details on a great day out at Torosay Castle & Gardens.

THE DUNDEE FLOWER SHOW 1996

FRIDAY 6 - SUNDAY 8 SEPTEMBER

CAMPERDOWN COUNTRY PARK

The Dundee Flower Show is widely regarded as one of the premier horticultural events in Scotland, attracting exhibitors from throughout the British Isles.

As at last year when we had over 15,000 visitors we will have a host of exhibition classes (over 1500) for flowers, fruit, vegetables, floral art, baking, preserves, handicrafts, wine and children's exhibits.

In addition, we have an extensive municipal displays area, a garden fair for plants and sundries, a craft fair and food fair for Scottish produce.

Each day there are band concerts, entertainment for all the family, demonstrations and a quality range of catering with meals, snacks, ice cream and a licensed bar.

We look forward to seeing you in September at the show, in the magnificent setting of the parkland, lawns and gardens of Camperdown Mansion House.

TIMES

Friday 1.00 pm - 8.30 pm
Saturday 10.00 am - 8.00 pm
Sunday 10.00 am - 6.00 pm

Free Parking - City Wide Signing

CHARGES

Day Tickets - Adult...............................£3.00
Senior Citizens, Concessions,
Child...£2.00
Family (2 Adults and
3 Children maximum............................£7.00
3 Day Ticket..£6.00

For more information telephone 01382 - 434797

Discount on Admission
to the show.
Present on Admission.
1 Voucher per Person.

CITY OF DUNDEE
DISTRICT COUNCIL

PARKS

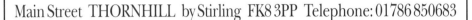
154

INDEX TO GARDENS

INDEX TO ADVERTISERS

160

Also available in the Cassell Education series:

P. Ainley and M. Corney: *Training for the Future: The Rise and Fall of the Manpower Services Commission*

G. Antonouris and J. Wilson: *Equal Opportunities in Schools*

N. Bennett and A. Cass: *From Special to Ordinary Schools*

M. Bottery: *The Morality of the School: The Theory and Practice of Values in Education*

C. Christofi: *Assessment and Profiling in Science*

G. Claxton: *Being a Teacher: A Positive Approach to Change and Stress*

C. Cullingford (ed): *The Primary Teacher*

B. Goacher *et al.*: *Policy and Provision for Special Educational Needs*

H. Gray (ed): *Management Consultancy in Schools*

L. Hall: *Poetry for Life*

J. Nias, G. Southworth and R. Yeomans: *Staff Relationships in the Primary School*

J. Sayer and V. Williams (eds): *Schools and External Relations: Managing the New Partnerships*

R. Straughan: *Beliefs, Behaviour and Education*

S. Wolfendale (ed): *Parental Involvement*